The Momen (Ulfat)

Family History

Prepared for the Momen Family Reunion
at De Poort, Groesbeek, Netherlands
13-16 July 2018

© Moojan Momen 2018
All Rights Reserved

The Momen (Ulfat) Family History / Moojan Momen

1. Momen (Ulfat) family. 2. Family history.
3. Baha'i Faith–history.

ISBN: 2370000460615
Nyon, Switzerland, 2018

Table of Contents

Foreword	3
Áqá Muhammad Husayn 'Attár Yazdí (Ulfat)	7
Fátimih-Sughrá	41
Prayer and Tablet of 'Abdu'l-Bahá	65
Khadíjih Ulfat	69
Sakínih Ulfat	79
'Alí Ulfat	83
Vadí'ih Momen	87
Muhammad Labib	91
Mahboubeh Kouchekzadeh	97
Sedratollah Momen	109
Eshghollah Momen	117
Zoghollah Momen	123
Majzoubeh Behrouzmand	133
Mahin Vahdat	139
Farid Vahdat's Imprisonment	147
Family Genealogy	157
Photographs	181

Foreword

The compilation of genealogies and family histories is an activity that has become very popular in recent years. It is often part of a quest for identity. In previous ages, it was thought worthwhile to record the lives of only the notables of a society. And so many ordinary people did not even think of recording the stories of their own families. Stories about the family were handed down verbally however and it was usually the women in families who were the custodians of these stories.

For this family, the writing down of its history is especially important because the family has migrated from its country of origin and settled in all parts of the world. At the forthcoming family reunion in the Netherlands, it is expected that family members will come from three continents and twelve countries. Thus for the younger generations of the family, the culture and environment of Iran where the family originated will become increasingly distant and unfamiliar. By recording the stories of the family at this time, a link with that past can be maintained and information can be preserved that would inevitably otherwise be lost.

The research that led to this book started in the summer of 1970, when I was able to record in Tehran the memories of my great-aunt Khadíjih Ulfat (who in our family we always called Khaleh Khanum) on a cassette recorder with fading batteries belonging to Farshid Momen. Although she was in her nineties and almost bedbound, her mind was sharp and her memories of the events of the 1903 perscution of the Bahá'ís in Yazd streamed from her mouth without hesitation.

Then in 1979, I went with my family and Mahboubeh Kouchekzadeh to London Airport to meet Muhammad Labib on a stopover from USA to Iran. He urged me to translate his book *The Seven Martyrs of Hurmuzak* as a way of demonstrating that the Bahá'ís were not favoured and protected by the previous Pahlavi government as was being said as part of the propaganda against the Bahá'í Faith by the Islamic revolutionary government of Iran. When he reached Iran, he sent me as well as *The Seven Martyrs of Hurmuzak*, his record of his sixty-day pilgrimage with his father to the presence of 'Abdu'l-Bahá. This book gave much information about the early history of the family.

I began to write this history in the late 1990s. The tapes from Khadíjih Ulfat were difficult to understand both due to the fact that the batteries on the cassette recorder had run down while recording and when the tape was played back at correct speed the words were slow and slurred. And the very thick Yazdi accent of Khadíjih Ulfat added to the problems. The first problem was solved by my son Sedrhat who was able to speed up the slow part of the tape so that it sounded more or less normal. The second part of the problem was solved in 2001, when I travelled on two occasions to Madrid to visit Mahin Vahdat, who had listened to Khadjih Khanum all her life and was familiar with the Yazdi accent and use of words. She was able to transcribe the words of the tape.

Later, I also taped interviews with Mahin Vahdat herself, who is a mine of information about the family, and Zoghollah Momen and Farid Vahdat, especially about their imprisonment. In addition, my mother Gloria Momen located and sent from time to time Tablets addressed to various members of the family. I have also received some reminiscences and notes from Muhammad 'Ali Razavi, Nika Vahdat, Nirvana Fleming and Farshid and Guitty Momen as well as photographs and answers from many people to emailed questions I have sent over the years. These and other resources have formed the basis of this book. Carmel Momen, Hooman Momen and Ashley Southall have assisted with the production of this book.

> Moojan Momen
> Bedfordshire, England
> 14 May 2018

Áqá Muhammad Husayn 'Attár Yazdí (Ulfat)

Áqá Muhammad Husayn 'Attár Yazdí, who took the surname Ulfat and was called Áqá Buzurg by the younger generations of the family was born in 1232 AHSh/1853, the son of Muhammad Mahdí, a perfumer and pharmacist (*'attár*) of Yazd. His mother was Khadíjih Begum of Shiraz who was literate and educated. She lived to be about one hundred years of age. Áqá Muhammad Husayn followed his father's occupation and opened a pharmacy in the Chahár-Súq quarter of Yazd.[1] Other members of his family seem to have been in this business as his cousin (father's sister's son) was also an *'attár*. In about 1876, when he was about 23 years old, he married Fátimih-Sughrá and a year later their first child, a daughter, Khadíjih, was born.[2]

Áqá Muhammad Husayn was studious and read many books of religion and mysticism (*'irfán*). Through his reading and studies, he became attracted to the Shaykhí movement and after a time joined them. Since he was learned in religious matters and was a gifted speaker, he soon became very well-known and

---

1 Information mainly from the account by Jalal Ulfat in 'Azízullah Sulaymání, *Masabíh Hidáyat*, vol. 5 (Tehran: Mu'assisih Millí Matbu'át Amrí, 118 BE/1961), pp. 280-98.
2 By calculation from statements made by Khadíjih Ulfat in a recorded interview with Moojan Momen in summer 1970 in Tehran (henceforth: Khadíjih Ulfat interview). A transcript of this tape was made in January 2001 and April 2001 by Mahin Vahdat at the home of Nika Vahdat in Madrid, Spain.

well-respected among the Shaykhís. In the exposition of proofs and weighing up the rational and traditional sources of knowledge, he was very talented and he spoke in a clear and simple manner, which affected everyone who heard him.[3]

Áqá Muhammad Husayn became a Bahá'í in about 1882 when he was about 30 years of age. Fádil Mázandarání gives the date as being about 1300 AHQ (1882-3)[4] and the account of Muhammad Táhir Malmírí puts this event as being after Malmírí's return from Akka in about 1881. The story of how Áqá Muhammad Husayn became a Bahá'í has several versions which differ a little from each other. Hájí Muhammad Táhir Malmírí writes of the conversion of Muhammad Husayn Ulfat thus in his memoires:

> Áqá Muhammad Husayn Ulfat was one of the leaders of the Shaykhí sect and he was very firm in his opinions. Every day he would read the *Irshád al-'Awwám* [the book of the Shaykhí leader Hájí Muhammad Karím Khán Kirmání] for a group of the Shaykhis outside his pharmacy and he would explain it and comment on it. He would pray in the Shaykhi mosque. There was a certain Áqá Hasan, the son of Ustád Ahmad who was a Shaykhí but who had attended several Bahá'í meetings although he was not yet a declared believer. One day Áqá Muhammad Husayn Ulfat said to Áqá Hasan: "I have heard that this Táhir fellow (*Táhirak*) from Malmír is interfering in things and is inviting people to the Bábí religion. I would like one day to go to his

---

3   Information mainly from the account by Jalal Ulfat in Sulaymání, *Masabíh Hidáyat*, vol. 5, pp. 280-1.
4   Fádil Mázandarání, *Tárikh-i Zuhúr al-Haqq*, vol. 6, manuscript, pp. 839-40.

house and cut him down to size (*par u pút kuním*)."

Áqá Hasan immediately brought word of what had been said to me. I said to him: "Leave it two or three days. If he does not follow this up, then say to him: 'You said that you wanted to go to the house of this Táhir fellow. I would very much like to come with you.' Try in whatever way you can to get him to come, but not in a way that casts doubt on you." After a few days Áqá Hasan sent word that they had arranged to come to my house that night after they emerged from the mosque [i.e. after evening prayers]. It was winter and our reception room was very cold.

Anyway, an hour after sunset, they came to our house. We put some fire in the burner (*manqal*) and in due course we began to speak about the Faith. Our conversation extended until dawn. I asked Ulfat: "Have you eaten?" He said: "No, we thought we would soon return home, but little by little our going has been delayed." I said: "There is nothing in our home except some pieces of dry bread." He said: "Very well. Bring the dried bread." I brought three pieces of dried bread and a bowl of water. After that we began talking again. It became morning and after two hours of the day had passed, he said: "I must go and open my pharmacy, but I will come again tonight." When night fell, he came as promised. After sitting down, he asked: "What station does Hájí Muhammad Karím Khán have in this Cause." I replied: "Hájí Mírzá Muhammad Karím Khán has the position of being the point of darkness opposite the light." On hearing these words, he rose up immediately and said: "I will not remain here" and he quickly left the room.

But the next night he returned, although I did not think that he would ever return at all. When he had sat down, he said: "What was this thing that you said last night? On the first night, we sat talking all night and last night, as a result of what you said, I did not sleep all night. And besides this, I have not slept during the daytime either, for these last two days. So now tell me, what evidence do you have for what you have said?" I had memorised some verses from the Qur'an and some *hadiths*. I recited for him these verses of the Qur'an which are in the Surah of Smoke: "Verily the tree of Zaqqúm [a cursed tree in Hell] will be the food of the Sinful (*al-athím*). Like molten brass; it will boil in their insides - like the boiling of scalding water. (A voice will cry:) 'Seize ye him and drag him into the midst of the Blazing Fire! Then pour over his head the Penalty of Boiling Water; Taste thou (this)! Truly wast thou Mighty full of honour (*al-karím*)!'" (Qur'an 44:43-9).[5] And I explain this verse to him. And I also recited the hadith from ['Alí] the Commander of the Faithful in the book *Al-Durr al-Munazzam*, where he said: "The Mahdi and his age, and the Dajjál and his time, and the Sufyani and his emergence, and the Kirmání and his entry." "Hájí Muhammad Karím Khán is in the Qur'an with the name Karím and the title *athím* (sinful) and he is mentioned as the Kirmání in the blessed Tradition." Finally after some hours of talking, Áqá Muhammad Husayn said: "Very good. We have dealt with this as well." And he declared his faith and began to teach and guide other souls.[6]

---

5   In the version of Malmírí's memoires published in 'Azízullah Sulaymání, *Masabíh Hidáyat*, vol. 5, p. 285, Malmírí states that he also cited the reference to *athím* in Surah 45:7. The word *al-athím* was significant because Hájí Muhammad Karím Khán often referred to himself with a contrived humility as "*al-Athím*". See Baha'u'llah, *Kitáb-i-Íqán* (Wilmette: Bahá'í Publishing Trust, 1989), p. 190

6   Hájí Muhammad Táhir Malmírí, *Khátirát-i-Malamírí* (Baha'i-Verlag, Hofheim-Langenhain, 1992), pp. 99-101. This account is also published in 'Azízullah Sulaymání, *Masabíh Hidáyat,* vol. 5, pp. 283-6. The wording is slightly different, but there is little

Áqá Muhammad Husayn's grandson, Jalal Ulfat, wrote an account in which he related what he had heard his grandfather say:

> I was sitting in my shop one day, busy studying the *Irshád al-'Awwám*. One of my acquaintances came to me and when he saw that I was busy studying the Irshád al-'Awwám, he said: 'Why do you spend your time studying such a book? I have obtained a book that is several grades better and more beneficial than the *Irshád al-'Awwam*. Its author has also written something addressed to Haji Muhammad Karím Khan, the author of the Irshád al-'Awwam. If you wish I will bring it for you to read.' I replied: How can any book be more important than the *Irshád al-'Awwam*?' After some further conversation, it was decided that he would bring the book (this was the Kitáb-i Íqán and the Tablet addressed to Hájí Muhammad Kárím Khán, the Shaykhi leader, which Bahá'u'lláh has revealed). The next day, he was true to his word and brought me the Kitáb-i Íqán and the tablet and gave it to me with great respect. I read the tablet. Those divine words had such a great effect upon the depths of my soul and mind that it is not possible to describe it in the form of mere words. When I began reading the Kitáb-i Íqán, it caused me to understand the perplexing questions of the holy scriptures. I began gradually to be attracted and engaged by the Bahá'í teachings. I garnered from the harvest of spiritual knowledge (*'irfán*) and as a result accepted the Bahá'í religion. Before I became a believer in this great Cause, I had met on several occasions with Hájí Muhammad Táhir Malmírí, who

---

substantive difference.

was one of the famous and senior figures among the Bahá'ís of Yazd. I discussed and debated with him with much boldness and temerity. At our first session, I was not prepared to pay any heed to Malmírí's explanations. I was so proud of my own knowledge that I was not disposed to value his knowledge and virtues.[7]

Áqá Muhammad Husayn's daughter, Khadíjih, in an oral interview, recalled the conversion of her father thus:

> There were two people, Hájí Muhammad Táhir Malamírí and Mullá 'Abdu'l-Ghaní, who were teaching that they had discovered that the Qá'im had appeared and people went to them. Áqá Muhammad Ridá, who was martyred, and his brother Áqá Muhammad Ja'far were two who had gone and heard and investigated this. They came to my father and said there are such-and-such people – they did not say that they had gone to them – who have come and are saying that the Qá'im has appeared and are speaking about this. My father said: "Where are they? I will go and answer them in one minute. I will reply to their saying that the Qá'im has appeared. Where are they? I will go now." They said: "Let us go." My father went there and sat with Áqá Muhammad Táhir and Mullá 'Abdu'l-Ghaní and they spoke together. My father listened and gradually learned. In short, he went every night to them until he had investigated the matter and understood [i.e. became a Bahá'í]. Then he began to go to this person and that person [teaching]. He was a [Bahá'í] teacher. The people realised that he had turned back [on Islam].[8]

---

7 Cited in 'Azízullah Sulaymání, *Masabíh Hidáyat*, vol. 5, pp. 281-2.
8 Khadíjih Ulfat interview, transcript by Mahin Vahdat, pp. 13-14.

Thus when Áqá Muhammad Husayn Ulfat became a Bahá'í, he began to teach others about the new religion and soon became well-known to both the Bahá'ís and Muslims of Yazd as a Bahá'í teacher. Apart from his immediate family, his wife and children, none of the other members of his family appear to have become Bahá'ís however. When Áqá Muhammad Husayn became a Bahá'í he received a Tablet from Bahá'u'lláh. The following is a provisional translation:

> O Husayn! Arouse thyself, through the love of God and the flames of the fire of attraction to the All-Merciful, for the service of the Cause. In this day, whosoever wishes to serve must turn his back on whatsoever he has and must turn towards what is God's. O Husayn! In this day, the Sea of Generosity is billowing and the effulgences of the rays of the Sun of Bounty have encompassed the whole of existence. Whomsoever arises for the sake of God should not be seen sitting down nor standing still. With the hosts of utterance and with joy and radiance, he should give guidance to the wayward and strength to the weak.
>
> Let no soul be surprised at these lofty words. Jesus, the son of Mary, may peace be upon Him, observed a fisherman fishing. He said: "Leave your net and come and I will make you a fisher of men." After these words, although that man had stammered, now he became a speaker. Whereas he had been ignorant, now he came to the ocean of knowledge. Where he had been poor, now he found a way to the kingdom of wealth. Formerly, he had been lowly, now he reached the summit of grandeur. He had been lost, now he had attained to the lights of the dawn of guidance. And when he had passed beyond the self and attached

himself to the True One, he burned his possessions in the fire of love and tore open the veils with the fingers of certitude. While he was in this world, he would say "O Spirit of God [Rúhu'lláh, i.e. Jesus Christ]!" and when he passed on to the next he attained a station which no pen can describe.

Well is it with those souls who today are not held back from Him who is the purpose of Creation by the doubts of those who repudiate Him nor the allusions of those who deny Him nor the turmoil raised by the people of the Bayán. Today is the day of fortitude and the day of service. Strive that haply you may achieve that which is worthy of mention before God and of being recorded in the Book. May the Glory (*bahá'*) be upon you and upon all who are firm and steadfast.[9]

Soon after his conversion, opposition to Áqá Muhammad Husayn Ulfat's teaching of the Bahá'í Faith arose. In 1302/1884-5, about two years after he had become a Bahá'í, he was arrested by the Governor at the instigation of a number of Sayyids and imprisoned with stocks and chains. Repeatedly they bastinadoed his feet and the prison warders would not allow his wife to visit. Khadíjih Ulfat was about seven years old at this time. She describes what happened:

> They came to my father's shop from the citadel. The governor sent them to go to the shop of Husayn-i Bábí and bring him. They went there, Ghulám-'Alí the black and some others, I don't know whom. They said "come here" and slapped him several times, dragging him from one end of his shop to the other and taking

---

9   Provisional translation of a Tablet of Bahá'u'lláh published in 'Azízullah Sulaymání, *Masabíh Hidáyat*, vol. 5, pp. 286-7.

him to the prison until the next day. The next day, they brought him out again and beat him with pomegranate tree branches until his feet were covered in sores.

One day – I do not know whether I was seven years old at the time or six that I remember these things – my grandfather came to our house. There was myself and the second of us the mother of Dr Ulfat [Sakínih Khanum], and the third was your uncle ['Alí Ulfat]. We were sitting down and our eyes were hurting. In those days, pain in the eyes was very common. My mother came, washed her hands and laid down a carpet – it was cold. She put the carpet down in the sun and said: "sit down here". My grandfather said: "You sit down here, children. I am going to get your father." Grandfather went into the room where there was a handkerchief full of money. He came out again and said: "Children, I am just going to get your father." This was after 14 or 15 days. Then he went.

We were saying: "Our father is coming, our father is coming." Then after a time, we saw our father coming with our grandfather. There was a very large courtyard. Our father came and sat down and held each of us in his arms and kissed us. We sat in his arms. We had three paternal aunts with whom we shared the house. Our three aunts came, as well as my grandfather and my mother and they all sat down. Then my father pulled up his trouser legs. His legs were just a mass of blood. This is one of the memories of my childhood – my father showing his legs to my mother and his sisters and saying: "Each day, they would bring me out once and tie my feet to a stool and beat them with the branches of the pomegranate tree. Then they would take me and throw me back into the prison. My feet were like pieces of meat, but they would beat them for a time. As soon as they got a little better, it would be time for them to bring me out and beat me again. This was the regular routine of their work."[10]

After one month, because his teaching of the Bahá'í Faith to the prisoners was beginning to have results, he was freed, after the payment of a large sum of money and the intercession of the Nawwabs. Again, when the governorship changed, this stirred up the enemies of the Faith and he was fined.

One memorable meeting at which Áqá Muhammad Husayn was present was in 1306/1888, when Mírzá Abu'l-Fadl Gulpáygání was visiting Yazd. During this visit, he had a meeting with Shaykh Muhammad Yazdí, who was a supporter of Azal and had been mixing with the Bahá'ís of Yazd, trying to throw doubts into their minds and to persuade them of the truth of the Azalí position. The meeting was held at the home of one of the Bahá'ís whom Shaykh Muhammad had thrown into doubt. Also present were 'Andalíb, who had come with Mírzá Abu'l-Fadl, and Áqá Muhammad Husayn 'Attar. Hájí Mírzá Haydar 'Alí Isfahání, who records this meeting in his biography of Gulpáygání, writes the following description of Áqá Muhammad Husayn:

> Also present was Áqá Muhammad Husayn 'Attar who is one of those who are firm, steadfast, well assured, who have prostrated themselves in the dust of the sacred threshold, and have a manner of speaking and powers of explanation that are truly the inspiration and confirmation of the All-Powerful, and whose numerous gifts of heavenly virtues and divine attributes both pen

---

10 Khadíjih Ulfat interview, transcript by Mahin Vahdat, pp. 17-18

and speech are powerless to describe.¹¹

In this debate, Shaykh Muhammad was defeated by the arguments of Mírzá Abu'l-Fadl and began to curse and abuse the Bahá'ís saying the Bahá'ís followed no law and had no morals. Although Mirza Abu'l-Fadl tried to calm the meeting down, Shaykh Muhammad became more excitable and began making exaggerated statements. Eventually, 'Andalíb could bear it no more and got up saying, "These are all lies and fabrications." At this Shaykh Muhammad got up and said, "This is not a meeting for discussion, it is a field of battle." Mírzá Abu'l-Fadl tried to get him to sit down so that the meeting would not end in bitterness and recriminations and so that the owner of the house would be guided to the truth. But Shaykh Muhammad would not be mollified and left. Áqá Muhammad Husayn got up and hurried after him, trying to persuade him to return, but to no avail. But the house-owner, who had been out of the room while this interchange was going on returned and expressed satisfaction at the fact that Shaykh Muhammad had left and that he had seen quite enough to realise what the truth was. Shortly after this meeting Shaykh Muhammad left Yazd.

During the 1891 persecutions that resulted in the Seven Martyrs of Yazd, Áqá Muhammad Husayn was persecuted and imprisoned (see also Khadíjih Ulfat's account of this below). ¹²

In 1315/1897-8, Áqá Muhammad Husayn went on

---

11   Haji Mirza Haydar 'Ali Isfahani, *Tarjumih-yi Ahvál-i Abu'l-Fadá'il* (photocopied manuscript in the Afnan Library), p. 388.
12   Fádil Mázandarání, *Tárikh-i Zuhúr al-Haqq*, vol. 6, p. 840.

pilgrimage to Akka and spent some time in the presence of 'Abdu'l-Bahá.[13] He continued his teaching of the Bahá'í Faith both by day at his shop and by night at meetings held for enquirers. His teaching guided many to the Faith but also aroused the anger and resentment of the enemies of the Faith, such that the Bahá'í historian Fádil Mázandarání writes about the 1903 upheaval in Yazd: "One major causes of that upheaval was the fact that the people were angry at his [Áqá Muhammad Husayn's] teaching."[14]

The 1903 upheaval began in Yazd with the arrival of Sayyid Ibráhím, a new Friday Prayer leader (*imám-jum'ih*) who came from Karbala. A group of the townspeople went out of the town to meet and greet Sayyid Ibrahim at Hájiyábád. He immediately began talking to them about what he had just witnessed in Isfahan: that there had been a general upheaval against the Bahá'ís and two people had been killed. The Bahá'í historian Sayyid Abu'l-Qásim Qummí Yazdí, known as Baydá, who compiled the fullest account that we have of the 1903 persecution of the Bahá'í in Yazd, writes:

> First he [Sayyid Ibráhím] had asked about the preeminent (*'umdah*) person among the Bahá'ís Áqá Muhammad Husayn 'Attár and whether he was still in Yazd. They had replied to him: 'Yes, he is well and is determinedly teaching [the Bahá'í Faith] in Yazd.' That infidel had commented 'We shall have to put that right.'[15]

---

13   Fádil Mázandarání, *Tárikh-i Zuhúr al-Haqq*, vol. 6, p. 840.
14   Fádil Mázandarání, *Tárikh-i Zuhúr al-Haqq*, vol. 6, p. 840.
15   Sayyid Abu'l-Qásim Baydá, *Tárikh-i Baydá* (ed. Siyamak Zabihi-Moghaddam, Hofheim: Bahá'i-Verlag, 2016), p. 25

Sayyid Ibrahim arrived in Yazd on Saturday 12 June 1903. Rumours began to circulate that he came with a decree (*fatvá*) from Sayyid Muhammad Kázim [Yazdí] Hujjat al-Islám, one of the leading *mujtahids* of the Shi'i world, for the massacre of the Bahá'ís. Although the *fatvá* was never produced and probably never existed, the whole episode produced an air of excitement in the town. Among the clerics who agitated against the Bahá'ís during those days was Mírzá Muhammad Písh-Namáz, the prayer leader in the Minár Mosque. He specifically called for the killing of Áqá Muhammad Husayn. Another was Mullá Ibráhím, the prayer leader of the Mosque of the Fahhádán quarter, who gave a verbal *fatvá* for the killing of Áqá Muhammad Husayn.[16]

The following day, 17 Rabí' al-Avval (13 June), was day on which the Shí'ís celebrate the birthday of the prophet Muhammad. Large crowds gathered at the house of Sayyid Ibráhím and he again spoke of what had happened in Isfahan and incited the crowd.

> In that gathering, the wicked people of the Abu'l-Qasim Quarter were present. They asked: "Áqá, what shall we do?" He had replied: "Go and bring Áqá Muhammad Husayn 'Attár, and those like him, to this gathering so that we can interrogate him and give him his full punishment." Those wicked people who consisted of well-known criminal elements (*alvát*) emerged from the house of the Imám [-Jum'ih] and went to find weapons such as knives and guns. That afternoon they went to the Chahár Súq in the citadel part of the town, to the door of the shop of Áqá Muhammad Husayn 'Attár,

---
16 Sayyid Abu'l-Qásim Baydá, *Tárikh-i Baydá*, p. 42.

intending to capture him and take him to the Imám[-Jum'ih]. As it happened, at that hour, Áqá Muhammad Husayn was not in the shop. It is reported that he had gone to the assembly of consultation.[17] [The crowd then went on and looted several other Bahá'í shops in that quarter]. The son of Áqá Muhammad Husayn, Áqá 'Alí, as soon as the trouble started, had left the shop and fled.[18]

The next day, the rabble came to the home of Áqá Muhammad Husayn. Khadíjih Ulfat records:

> There were two streets and the house of Hájí Muhammad Ismá'íl was between the two. One street went up one side [of the house] and the other street went up the other. As the mob approached our house, they did not recognise my father and brother as they were leaving. As they were going down one side, the mob was coming up the other and so they were able to pass them and go on.[19]

The rabble reached the home of Áqá Muhammad Husayn:

> Javad 'Attar who was a relative of Áqá Muhammad Husayn and lived next door, came and brought some oil and a flame so they could set fire to the door of the house. The family of Áqá Muhammad Husayn, realising what was happening, started to pour water from behind and over the top of the door. It was towards evening that a government official (*farráshbáshí*) and

---

17 *Mahfil-i Shawr*, forerunner of the local Spiritual Assembly.
18 Baydá, *Táríkh-i Baydá*, pp. 26-7.
19 Khadíjih Ulfat interview, transcript by Mahin Vahdat, p. 11.

some attendants came and the mob dispersed.[20]

For two days the mob rampaged through the streets until, on 15 June, the first martyrdom occurred, that of Áqá Mírzá-yi Halabí-sáz. Áqá Muhammad Husayn went to the home of one of the Bahá'ís, Áqá Mírzá Husayn Sha'rbáf, and hid there. All the Bahá'ís thought that the governor would soon reassert his authority and the trouble would blow over.

Then things quietened for a few days. But news arrived that in Taft and Ardikan, two towns in the region of Yazd, there had been anti-Bahá'í persecutions and some Bahá'ís had been killed. Áqá Muhammad Husayn was visiting Sayyid Abu'l-Qásim Qummí Yazdí, known as Baydá, when this news arrived and it was thought to be unsafe to go out onto the streets, so he stayed the night there.[21]

The governor summoned Mírzá Mahmúd Afnán (son of Mírzá Muhammad Taqi Afnán, a cousin of the Báb, who had been the Russian consular agent in Yazd). He said that he feared that the situation in Yazd could get out of hand and urged that the well-known Bahá'ís should be sent out of Yazd, and those who could not go should be kept concealed. According to Fádil Mázandarání, the Imám-Jum'ih himself was saying: "I will myself cut off the head of Áqá Muhammad Husayn with a saw."[22] Malmírí writes that upon Mírzá Mahmúd Afnán's return from his interview with the Prince Governor, he acted immediately:

---

20 Baydá, *Táríkh-i Baydá*, p. 31.
21 Baydá, *Táríkh-i Baydá*, p. 43.
22 Fádil Mázandarání, *Táríkh-i Zuhúr al-Haqq*, vol. 6, pp. 840.

[Mírzá Mahmúd Afnán] sent for Áqá Muhammad Husayn 'Attár, who was one of the prominent Bahá'í teachers of the town and was concealed in the home of Áqá Mírzá Husayn Sha'rbáf, who is one of the firm Bahá'ís. He consulted with him and with some of the other Bahá'ís who had gathered in this house. They agreed to the departure of some of the well-known Bahá'ís, as requested by the Governor, for they realised that little by little the situation was deteriorating.[23]

Áqá Muhammad Husayn transferred to the Afnáns' complex of buildings. The Afnáns had brought men with rifles from the villages that they owned in Bavanat in Fars. Khadíjih Ulfat records:

My father went to the house of the Shirázís [Afnáns]. They had called for the Bavánátís to come to the town. Bavánát is near Shiraz. They had come, each one of them with a rifle, and gone onto the roof of the house so that if any [of the mob] approached the house, they would fire on them. No-one approached the house. After a time, they [the Afnáns] called together these men [the Bavánátís] and my father and said: "We are entrusting Áqá Muhammad Husayn into your hands. If one hair on his head is harmed, we will hold you responsible. Take him with you and give him clothes and a mantle and whatever is needed so that he is not recognised." So they took him – there was a large group of them – and they went to Bavánát of Shiraz. They were used to

---

23 Hájí Muhammad Táhir Malmírí, *Tárikh Shuhadá-yi Yazd*, pp. 113-14. There is some discrepancy in that Bayda (*Tárikh-i Baydá*, p. 82) states that Áqá Muhammad Husayn was in his house when word came from Mírzá Mahmúd Afnán, while this account by Malmírí says that he was in Áqá Mírzá Husayn Sha'rbáf's house.

wandering in the desert and were agriculturalists. He [Áqá Muhammad Husayn] related: "I was seated on a donkey and I had a handkerchief in my hand. I was crying. What has happened to my children? Where are they now?"[24]

Another person who was removed from Yazd alongside Ulfat was Mírzí Mahmúd Zarqání. The party left on 26 June 1903.[25] According to Malmírí and Mázandarání, Áqá Muhammad Husayn was in Bavánát for some two or three months, and supported himself as a pedlar, before the situation had calmed down sufficiently in Yazd for him to return.[26] As his own home had been destroyed, he returned to the Afnán's home.[27] Khadíjih Ulfat records:

> When the turmoil had settled a little, my father returned to the Afnán's house. From there he sent for my mother and they were able to see each other again. Then I do not know how long it was, perhaps a month, that his arms and legs became swollen. They brought him to the house of his son-in-law ("Hájí Mírzá Dámád", the father of Dr Ulfat). We were all together there. My father came and sat.
> Night by night, a doctor was brought to my father. He said: "Eat a little deer meat, grilled." He would give a prescription and leave by night. I do not

---

24 Khadíjih Ulfat interview, transcript by Mahin Vahdat, p. 11.
25 Fádil Mázandarání, *Tárikh-i Zuhúr al-Haqq*, vol. 8, part 1, p. 565.
26 Hájí Muhammad Táhir Malmírí, *Khátirát-i-Malamírí*, p. 101, Fádil Mázandarání, *Tárikh-i Zuhúr al-Haqq*, vol. 6, p. 840.
27 Fádil Mázandarání states that it was actually to the Afnán's farm in the village of Mihdiyábád, just outside Yazd, that Áqá Muhammad Husayn returned, *Tárikh-i Zuhúr al-Haqq*, vol. 6, p. 840.

know how long it was that my father was in the house. They were saying that it is the swelling of dropsy that has blown up his hands and feet. He had the medicines and became a little better.[28]

Áqá Muhammad Husayn now had to contemplate his future. His home had been completely wrecked. Not only had the contents been destroyed or looted, but the mob had even carried away some of the bricks. His business had been destroyed, the contents of his shop were either looted or rendered worthless. According to Fádil Mázandarání, those who owed him money refused to pay their debts and those to whom he owed money pressed him to pay.[29] But much worse was the fact that his wife had been publicly stripped of her head-dress and veil (see history of Fátimih-Sughrá, below). It is difficult for those who have no experience of the society in which Áqá Muhammad Husayn lived to understand the enormity of the humiliation of his wife being publicly stripped of her head-dress and veil. It meant that the family could not remain in Yazd (for discussion of this issue see history of Fátimih-Sughrá). And so it was suggested to Áqá Muhammad Husayn that he move to Tehran. Khadíjih Ulfat recalls:

> The daughter and son-in-law of Mírzá Mahmúd Afnán were moving to 'Ishqábád and Jalál ad-Dawlih had been dismissed as Governor of Yazd and been told to leave the town. So Hájí Mírzá Mahmúd and his family, together with Jalál ad-Dawlih, were all departing.

---

28 Khadíjih Ulfat interview, transcript by Mahin Vahdat, pp. 11-12.
29 Fádil Mázandarání, *Tárikh-i Zuhúr al-Haqq*, vol. 6, p. 840.

It was suggested that when they left, he [Áqá Muhammad Husayn] should go with them. Thus Hájí Mírzá Mahmúd and Jalál ad-Dawlih came to Tehran and brought my father with them here to the house of Arbáb Jamshíd with [Áqá] Siyávash. They [Hájí Mírzá Mahmúd and his family] then went on to 'Ishqábád.[30]

Áqá Muhammad Husayn at first stayed at the house of Arbáb Jamshíd, a wealthy Zoroastrian entrepreneur who had several Bahá'ís, such as Áqá Siyávash, working for him. Áqá Muhammad Husayn also began to work for Arbáb Jamshid and was supervisor of all of his most important affairs.[31] Eventually, either when Arbab Jamshid was bankrupted in 1913 or when Áqá Muhammad Husayn had accumulated enough money, he started a pharmacy in a small caravanserai known as the Tímchih-yi Hájib ad-Dawlih. After two or three years[32] he sent for his wife, his two sons ('Alí and Muhammad) and his youngest daughter (Vadí'ih) to come to Tehran. His two older daughters had already married and remained with their husbands.

Arbáb Jamshíd gave them a house to live in near the Darvázih-yi Dawlat (Government Gate of the city) behind the gardens of the Amír A'zam. Its rooms were large but its courtyard was small.[33]

After another three or four years, Áqá Muhammad

---

30 Khadíjih Ulfat interview, transcript by Mahin Vahdat, p. 12.
31 Fádil Mázandarání, *Tárikh-i Zuhúr al-Haqq*, vol. 8, part 2, p. 951.
32 Khadíjih Ulfat says it was after three years; Khadíjih Ulfat interview, transcript by Mahin Vahdat, p. 13. Muhammad Labib says it was after two years, *Khatirát-i Shast Rúzih*, manuscript, p. 7.
33 Khadíjih Ulfat interview, transcript by Mahin Vahdat, p. 12.

Husayn, concerned that his grandson (Jalál Ulfat, the son of his daughter Khadíjih) was not being educated, sent for him also to come to Tehran so that he could attend the Tarbiyat Bahá'í School that had just opened.[34]

'Abdu'l-Bahá sent several tablets consoling the family for the suffering that they had sustained in the course of the persecutions in Yazd. A provisional translation of one of these reads:

> He is God!
> O Attár! Praise be to God that thou art spreading the musk-like fragrances and the evidence for this is your endurance of countless trials and tribulations. You are content with the Almighty and occupied, day and night, with being grateful for the favours of God the Omnipotent. This is evidence that you are deserving of every bounty and worthy of all love. I ask of God that he decree for you that a mighty recompense and a favourable end may appear from this calamity. Upon you be greetings and praise. 'Ayn 'Ayn.[35]

After the First World War had ended, Áqá Muhammad Husayn and his younger son, Muhammad Labib went on pilgrimage to meet 'Abdu'l-Bahá in Haifa. They arrived in Haifa on 8 October 1919 and remained in the Holy Land for 60 days, meeting with 'Abdu'l-Bahá on more than 70 occasions. Their fellow-pilgrims included such figures as the Hand of the Cause Ibn Asdaq, the future Hands of the Cause Dr John Esslemont and 'Azízu'llah Varqá, and such persons as Dr Lutfullah Hakim, Fadil Mazandarani and Harry Randall. Muhammad Labib

---

34 Khadíjih Ulfat interview, transcript by Mahin Vahdat, p. 12.
35 Muhammad Labib, *Khatirát-i Shast Rúzih*, manuscript, p. 7.

has written a detailed record of those days, which it is not possible even to summarize here. According to Muhammad Labib, their going was in part the result of an error:

> In the year 76, equivalent to 1919, . . . a telegraph in English, with 'Abdu'l-Bahá's signature, arrived from the Holy Land addressed to the Tehran Spiritual Assembly. It said: "The presence in the Holy Land of Mazandarani, Yazdi and Labib is necessary. 'Abbas."
> Later it transpired that in place of Yazdi and Labib, 'Abdu'l-Bahá had meant two other people, but as a result of the switching around and deletion of some letters in the telegram, in the course of transmission, it had come out in this form.[36]

According to another source, during World War I, Mírzá Ahmad Yazdání had written to the Central Organization for a Durable Peace about the Bahá'í teachings and had suggested that for further information, they should refer to 'Abdu'l-Baha. 'Abdu'l-Baha received a letter from them after the war and telegrammed to Tehran that Ibn Asdaq and Yazdani should proceed at once to Haifa. In the course of transmission, however, the name of Yazdani had been changed to that of Yazdi. The only prominent Bahá'í of Tehran known as Yazdi was Áqá Muhammad Husayn and so it was decided that he should leave immediately for Haifa. He left with his son Muhammad

---

36 Muhammad Labib, *Khatirát-i Shast Rúzih*, manuscript, p. 42; according to Fádil Mazandarani, *Zuhuru'l-Haqq*, vol. 8, part 2, pp. 859-60, the telegram from 'Abdu'l-Bahá to the Bahá'ís of Rasht had asked "Shahíd, Mazandarani and Yazdání" to come to Haifa, but in the course of transmission, Yazdani had changed to Yazdi, and so it was thought that Ulfat was intended.

Labib and Ibn Asdaq.[37]

After the pilgrimage, 'Abdu'l-Bahá sent a tablet in his own hand-writing to Áqá Muhammad Husayn in which he wrote (a provisional translation):

> O pilgrim who circles around the Concourse on High! Praise be to God that with divine assistance and grace you completed those distant stages, traversed deserts and arrived at your destination. It is not possible to imagine a bounty greater than attaining to that threshold. Be thankful to the Almighty Lord that this was your lot.[38]

In Tehran, Áqá Muhammad Husayn purchased a house in the Kúchih Malik near what used to be the Siráh-yi Sháh. At the end of the road was a school, the Madrasih Khayriyyih built by Muntazam ad-Dawlih Firuzábádí, which was later called the Madrasih Firuzábádí. Across the road from the plot of land purchased by Áqá Muhammad Husayn was empty land that was later purchased by other members of the family and built upon. Áqá Muhammad Husayn wanted to buy some land behind that house for a house for his son-in-law, Muhammad Momen, but a price could not be agreed upon. Several of his grandchildren lived with him so that they could obtain an education at the Bahá'í schools in Tehran – because their parents were not in Tehran. We have already noted Jalál Ulfat above. Mahboubeh Momen (Kouchekzadeh) was another while her parents were posted in various parts of Iran. Abbas Sabet (Thabit)

---

37 'Azizu'llah Sulaymani, *Masábih Hidáyat*, vol. 9 (Tehran: Mu'assisih Matbú'át Amrí, 132 BE/1975), pp. 357-8.
38 Muhammad Labib, *Khatirát-i Shast Rúzih*, manuscript, p. 42.

was a neighbour and he describes his memories of that household:

> [After leaving Yazd], they lived (in Tehran) in great poverty and penury, but the light of faith and the fire of love shone forth from their faces in that house. We were friends and neighbours and thus were constantly in each other's houses. There was much joy and pleasure in the interactions between our two households. We were only separated by a short distance and a wall. Our two households were so interwoven through friendship that sometimes they were in our house and helping us with our affairs and sometimes we were in their house, joyfully and without any reservations helping them and thus our days were spent.
>
> I will never forget those moon-lit spring nights in that street, which did not yet have electric lighting. The moon would be shining brightly and its rays would glint through the leaves of the acacia tree (*aqáqiyá*), which was covered from top to bottom in blossom and from which emanated a heart-alluring fragrance, and it would shine onto the meal that we had spread out. The meal that was spread out was very simple, having no elaborate sauces (*khoresh*) on it. It consisted just of a delicious bread, yoghurt, cheese and herbs. Sometimes as many as ten or fifteen people would, with the utmost joy, sit around the table-cloth, shoulder to shoulder, face to face. It was as though it were a table sent from heaven, shining in light of love and affection.[39]

Áqá Muhammad Husayn quickly established himself, both as a highly regarded business man with his

---

39 'Abbás Thábit, "Bih Yád Du Tan az Muballighín Amru'lláh", *Payám Bahá'í*, no. 228 (Nov. 1998) p. 51.

pharmacy and as a prominent Bahá'í teacher. 'Azízu'lláh Sulaymání remembers meeting him when he came to Tehran in 1301 AHSh/1924:

> This servant was able to meet him in Tehran in 1301 AHSh/1924 and benefit from his intellectually and spiritually nourishing discourse. At that time he had a pharmacy store in the Sará-yi Hájib ad-Dawlih. The merchants in that small caravanserai, despite the fact that they knew that he was one of the most important people to whom the Bahá'ís turned, nevertheless had complete trust in him. Whenever any of them was absent, they would plead and insist that he should weigh their tea or their other trading goods, so confident were they that if he supervised such matters, there would be no deception.[40]

Áqá Muhammad Husayn was famed among the Bahá'ís as a teacher of the Faith. He was known for his skill in debate and discussion. Abbas Sabet was a neighbour and writes of Áqá Muhammad Husayn thus:

> He was one of those souls who spent their days and their nights in teaching the Faith. In 1903, in the deadly upheaval in Yazd, he had narrowly escaped the sharp claws and blood-drenched teeth of the enemies of the Faith. He became a refugee and came to Tehran. Our family were neighbours to this family and we lived down the same lane (in one of the roads branching off Pahlavi Street). After Áqá Muhammad Husayn came to Tehran, he opened, with a small outlay of capital, a pharmacy in the bazaar. After a time he left that occupation and spent his whole time in teaching and

---

40 'Azízullah Sulaymání, *Masabíh Hidáyat*, vol. 5, p. 278.

spreading the Cause of God. He spoke engagingly. With proofs from the Qur'an and verses from Mawlavi (Rúmí), he would fill those who were enquiring about the Faith with joy and would make them aware of their innermost self. And if the enquirer were just, he would lead that person to the pure wellspring of faith. Many of the notables and enquirers of Zoroastrian origin were taught the Faith by him.[41]

Among those who benefited from Bahá'í classes that Áqá Muhammad Husayn taught at the Afsahí house was Jalál Khazeh, the future Hand of the Cause:

> In his (Jalál Khazeh's) childhood at his mother's suggestion, he attended each week two teaching gatherings, one was the meetings of the late Mirza 'Ali Akbar Rafsanjání, held in the home of Aqa Hasan Qassáb Muhájirín, and the other was the meetings of the late Áqá Muhammad Husayn Ulfat, held in the home of the late Afsáhi. He considered that his coming to believe in the Cause of the Abhá Beauty was owing to the guidance of his mother and his participation in these teaching meetings.[42]

Áqá Muhammad Husayn was often called upon to deal with those who came to Bahá'í meetings for the purpose of disruption or with difficult and clever arguments against the Bahá'í Faith. Hand of the Cause Mr Abu'l-Qasim Faizi said that the Bahá'ís would always take

---

41 'Abbás Thábit, *Taríkhchih-yi Madrasih-yi Tarbiyat-i Banín* (New Delhi: Mirat Press, 1997), p. 224.
42 Autobiographical account by Jalal Khazeh in 'Abdu'l-'Ali 'Ala'i, *Mu'assisih Ayádí Amru'lláh* (Tehran: Mu'assisih Millí Matbú'át Amrí), 130/1973, p. 688.

their most difficult enquirers to him and he would either convert them or silence them.⁴³ 'Azizu'llah Sulaymani writes:

> In the time of Ulfat, as at other times, the well-known and serving teachers of the Bahá'í Faith resided in Tehran. Some of them were ready to cope with any intellectual trickery. Thus if it became necessary to deal with a quarrelsome or hypocritical or sarcastic individual in such a way as to bring him to his knees in a debate, Ulfat would be suggested for this. He would engage in a discussion with this individual and within about quarter of an hour would render him powerless and defeated, unable to even speak or ask a question. What a pity that none of his sessions of debate were recorded so that they could be studied and it would be known how skilful Ulfat was in speech and exposition and how he adjusted his introductory remarks so as to achieve a precise goal at the end. It was for this reason that those enquirers who were truly seeking regarded him as invaluable and eagerly sought his presence, while argumentative and prejudiced individuals, when they had come across him once and experienced his strength of argument, avoided coming up against him again.⁴⁴

The Hand of the Cause Abu'l-Qasim Faizi related in a talk one episode in which a particularly vehement advocate of the philosophy of materialism had been troubling the Bahá'ís:

---

43 Notes by Moojan Momen from a conversation with Mr Faizi at Tiverton Summer School in England, 21 August 1975.
44 'Azízullah Sulaymání, *Masabíh Hidáyat*, vol. 5, pp. 278-9.

The time of Áqá Muhammad Husayn Yazdí was one in which the youth would go off to Europe and learn three or four languages and study various subjects. Then they would return to Iran and come to Bahá'í firesides and speak the utmost rubbish. For example one of them said [in response to an exposition of the Bahá'í teachings]: "Sir what are you saying about God, we have attended laboratories over there [in Europe] and have looked into all aspects of the world, in physics and chemistry. We have looked into everything and have not seen God anywhere. We do not accept anything that we do not see." For one hour he went on with this. The Bahá'ís were boiling with frustration and anger. But Áqá Muhammad Husayn sat there, a mountain of patience and forebearance. His hand did not even come out of his *abá* [cloak]. Believe me when I say that he [the young man] went on for an hour. "We have studied the heavens and have knowledge of the stars. We have even gone beyond the heavens." We all sat there silent, not knowing what to say to the young man.

Áqá Muhammad Husayn sat there with a small hat on and his *abá* and did not appear to be taking any interest in what the man was saying. But then he raised his head and started speaking: "*Jánam, 'azízam* (my dear friend). Please do not be so disrespectful of your father and of your mother in front of this gathering." He repeated this two or three times. Everyone was astonished. The young man asked: "What relevance do your words have?" He replied: "Why do you maintain that a certain person is your father? Why do you say he is your father? How do you know? How did you come by this information? You did not see it. Perhaps it was someone else. So please do not say that I do not accept anything that I have not seen with my own eyes. You did not see this. Why then do you accept it?" Yes, he continued: "My dear friend, you know from the fact that this poor father of yours spent money on you, sent you to school, sent money to you over there [in Europe] so that you could study and become a human being. And now you return and say these things. Why do you insult your father?" This is how it was. Áqá Muhammad Husayn said: "There are many things that you accept but you have not seen this. For example you say that blood flows in the arteries and veins. Have you seen this? No, but you have sensed it. In the same way you have sensed that he [you father] has been kind to you, has given you a home, given you clothes. Every day he has given you the means to live, and so you accept that he is your father."

In this way Áqá Muhammad Husayn took the argument forward. He started to talk about the difference between the eye and vision. The eye is not the same as vision. The eye is just allows the transmition of the light. It itself does not see. The ability to see resides within the brain of the human being. You cannot see it. But as a result of this materialistic knowledge this becomes hidden. You need to step back a little. You will then see God in everything. This Áqá Muhammad Husayn was uneducated but everything he said was based on the Word of God.[45]

Another story told by Mr Faizi about the teaching abilities of Áqá Muhammad Husayn is as follows:

On one occasion in Najafábád, a man came to me and said: "They have said to me to come to the Bahá'í meeting and hear Áqá Muhammad Husayn Yazdí speak. But I do not want to come alone. I will bring a mujtahid with me." So the mujtahid came and sat

---

45 From a recording of a talk by Mr Faizi at the Hazírat al-Quds of Zargandih on 15/12/1354 AHSh.

down and Áqá Muhammad Husayn asked: "What do you have to share with us? Is there anything you want to say?" The mujtahid launched forth into a speech in refutation of the Faith. In the course of this, he said: I myself last night was given a mission by God and so I am a Messenger."

Áqá Muhammad Husayn rose and bowed and said "We have been waiting for such a Messenger. Give your proof and we will obey you. By what proof are you a Messenger of God? And what is your mission?" He replied: "My mission is to return all of the Bahá'ís to become Muslims again." Áqá Muhammad Husayn said: "Very well. Now, what proof do you have?" He said: "Whatever proofs you have for Bahá'u'lláh. I have those very same proofs."

Áqá Muhammad Husayn said: "We all who are Bahá'ís accept Bahá'u'lláh on one proof. And that proof is that Bahá'u'lláh said that every Messenger of God who has come before me is true. Now what do you say?"[46]

On another occasion, Mr Faizi related a story about Áqá Muhammad Husayn coming to a Bahá'í children's class which Mr Faizi was attending, although he was not a Bahá'í at the time.

> The teacher of that school got the various children to stand up and recite some prayers and tablets that they had memorised. Then Áqá Muhammad Husayn halted the proceedings by saying: "Useless!" Mr Faizi said that to this day he could remember what Áqá Muhammad Husayn said next, so powerfully did it impress itself

---

46 From a recording of a talk by Mr Faizi at the Hazírat al-Quds of Zargandih on 15/12/1354 AHSh.

upon his mind. He said: "This is like digging a hole in the sand and pouring water into it – it will all drain away. What you must do is to dig deep until you strike water which will then well up and give sweet water for all time." Mr Faizi then explained that you must dig deep into the mind of the child and bring out the spirituality that inherently exists, rather than trying to force the mantle of spirituality upon the child.[47]

'Abbas Sabet relates an episode in which Áqá Muhammad Husayn taught the Bahá'í Faith to a school-boy at the Tarbiyat school:

> These two boys took classes together and in the summer we would see them together by the "Áb Mangal" (a pool of drinkable water brought by *qanáts* – underground canals – to the city). I do not remember whether they were in the eighth form or the ninth form. One of them was a young Bahá'í boy from Isfahan and the other was a Muslim and from Tehran. The young Isfahani boy was truly a flame of fire and through his loving Bahá'í spirit had attracted his friend. Sometimes we would see those two youths with Áqá Muhammad Husayn seated on the bench outside the Malikzadeh house or seated by the side of a water channel. They would be speaking heatedly together for hours, until several hours of the night had passed. Eventually I heard from my brother that this young man had become a Bahá'í, but had come under severe interrogation and pressure from his ultra-religious mother and father.
>   One day his father asked him: "Who did you speak to?"

---

47 Notes by Moojan Momen from a conversation with Mr Faizi at Tiverton Summer School in England, 21 August 1975.

"To Áqá Muhammad Husayn."

Since this father and mother lived in the same quarter as we did, they knew Áqá Muhammad Husayn very well. So they said menacingly:

"May God curse this Satan of Yazd. We must turn him out of this quarter."

The boy was terrified and pleaded with his father, swearing an oath and saying: "It was I, of my own free will, who went to him"

His father continued saying to his son in angry tones: "If I don't kill him, then I will kill you, with your saying of Bábí prayers." The mother was standing next to her only child, her son, and she had tears streaming down her face.

Suddenly, the father, seized with bigotry and fanaticism, grasped a kitchen knife and took his son to a corner of the garden, intending to cut his throat there. But the mother, crying out, prevented her husband from doing this.[48]

Abbas Sabet goes on to describe how the boy, in despair, went to a pharmacist shop to purchase some mouse poison and then went to a ditch in a lonely spot and took it all. But the pharmacist was a Bahá'í and knew the boy's story and had guessed what was happening, so he only sold him a mild laxative. The next morning the distraught father and mother of the boy found him asleep in the ditch. When they realised what had happened they were very grateful to the pharmacist and eventually the whole family became Bahá'ís.[49]

Abbas Sabet describes Áqá Muhammad Husayn's

---

48 'Abbás Thábit, *Taríkhchih-yi Madrasih-yi Tarbiyat-i Banín*, pp. 204-5.
49 'Abbás Thábit, *Taríkhchih-yi Madrasih-yi Tarbiyat*, pp. 205-6.

personality thus:

> Áqá Muhammad Husayn was very sociable and because he had a very attractive way of speaking and a mellifluous tongue and he would intersperse his words with lines of meaningful poetry and stories. No-one would be wearied by him and he would always affect the hearts of those who heard him and awake them from their slumber. The seeds that he planted would slowly sprout and would in time become fruitful trees. In this way and following this method, he taught many and thus left behind an ever-lasting impression throughout the ages and centuries of himself and his faithful family.
>
> He was of relatively short stature and dark-complexioned with a half-grey beard. He always met people with a heart-felt smile that would give others hope. Whenever a discussion about the problems of life would arise in the course of discussion and someone would ask him his opinion, he would with a few words from the Bahá'í scriptures guide the other person. In his sweet Yazdí accent he would say: "In the [spiritual] world there is no sorrow, so do not allow sorrow into your life; there is nothing to be gained from it."[50]

Áqá Muhammad Husayn spent a great deal of his time studying the Bahá'í scriptures and much of the rest of it teaching the Bahá'í Faith. He also studied the *Fará'id* of Mirza Abu'l-Fadl as a guide to teaching. He travelled throughout Iran to teach the Bahá'í Faith. He is known to have gone to Qazvin, Hamadan, Kirmanshah, Rasht, Isfahan, Qumm, Yazd, Shahmirzad, Sangsar and, as the above story indicates, to Najafabad as well. He

---

50 'Abbás Thábit, "Bih Yád Du Tan az Muballighín Amru'lláh", *Payám Bahá'í*, no. 228 (Nov. 1998) pp. 51-2.

ÁQÁ MUHAMMAD HUSAYN 'ATTÁR YAZDÍ

was in great demand for Bahá'í "firesides" all over Tehran. Zoghollah, who went with him to a few of these, remembers that one fireside was at the house of Ziya'u'llah Seyhoun nearby, another was at the house of Afsahi in a distant part of town, another at the house of Mirza Nasír Khan; usually they would walk there. Mahin Vahdat remembers seeing him go out into the street to the side of the house and wait there in his abá. Ziya'u'llah Seyhoun would come by and pick him up on a bicycle and take him to the Bahá'í meetings. 'Abbas Sabet, who was a neighbour, writes:

> One can seldom remember Áqá Muhammad Husayn being at home at night. He would commit his wife, who had been ill since the time of the Yazd upheaval, to the care of the Blessed Beauty, his children and neighbours and, whether in summer or winter and despite the lack of means of transport in those days, he would set off by night to go a long way off to the houses where teaching meetings were being held, which in those days was often the houses of the Zoroastrians. He would sit until late at night and with his sweet talk would open up the ears and make his audience receptive to Bahá'í love. He would shine the candle of faith in their hearts so that those slumbering souls might be illumined by the rays of his light. Sometimes at dawn, when the cockrels of the morn were beginning to sing out their song, that sweet-singing bird would bring his talk to an end, and would make his way back to his nest.[51]

According to Mr Faizi, it was on one such trip to a Bahá'í meeting in Tehran in the cold of winter that he

---

51   'Abbás Thábit, "Bih Yád Du Tan az Muballighín Amru'lláh", *Payám Bahá'í*, no. 228 (Nov. 1998) p. 51.

contracted pneumonia,[52] as a result of which he died on 26 Urdibihisht 1315/16 May 1936.

---

[52] Notes by Moojan Momen from a conversation with Mr Faizi at Tiverton Summer School in England, 21 August 1975.

Fátimih-Sughrá

Fátimih-Sughrá was the wife of Áqá Muhammad Husayn Ulfat. She was also a native of Yazd. She was born in about 1860 and was about sixteen years of age when she was married in about 1876 to Áqá Muhammad Husayn who was then about 23 years of age. A year later, they had their first daughter, Khadíjih. In all, they had five children, three daughters and two sons: Khadíjih, Sakínih, 'Ali (who was named 'Alí Muhammad, and was therefore probably born after the conversion of his parents in about 1882), Ruqiyyih (who was later called Vadí'ih and was born in 1891) and Muhammad Mahdi (who was later called Muhammad Labíb and was born in 1893).

During the upheaval of the Seven Martyrs of Yazd in 1891, Fátimih-Sughrá had just given birth to her youngest daughter, Ruqiyyih (Vadí'ih). Khadíjih Ulfat, who at this time was about 14 years of age, recalled:

> Everyone was hiding because they were afraid. Our father (Áqá Muhammad Husayn) went to the house of the Shírázís (Afnáns). Then matters got a little better, because they restrained the people. When matters got a little easier, and people had begun coming out of their homes for two or three days, in fear and fright, they sent our servant Rubábih to say: "Áqá [Muhammad Husayn] asks that you come [to the house of the Afnáns] by night so that you can meet." But since Khánum Buzurg [Fátimih-Sughrá] had only just given birth, she replied:

"I cannot come now. When I have been to the baths, I will come." Then she [Rubábih] left, Khánum Buzurg went to the baths and then went there [to the house of the Afnáns].[53]

At the time of the 1903 upheaval in Yazd, the family were living in the Fahhádán or Yuzarún quarter of the city of Yazd in a house which was part of a cluster of seven houses. The other houses belonged to other members of the wider family. The houses were separate but the courtyards were connected with each other. Fátimih-Sughrá had 5 children by this time, ranging in age from nine years old to 26 years of age. The older two daughters had married and lived with their husbands. Khadíjih, the oldest daughter lived with her husband in the same cluster of houses of the family, but the other sister Sakínih lived in another quarter of the city. Fatimih-Sughra recounted the events of the start of this episode to Sayyid Abu'l-Qasim Baydá, which he recorded in his history:

> On Saturday night (13 June 1903), we took refuge in the [neighbouring] house of Áqa Javád 'Attár, who is a close relative and saw with our own eyes that from Friday afternoon to Saturday night, these blood-thirsty and evil people came, group after group, entering our house and looting it. They divided whatever clothes and other things that were in the house among themselves and took them away. With the utmost courage and forbearance, we were occupied with reciting the words of God. I had some small children, aged three and nine.[54] They were also in the house and observed these

---

53 Khadíjih Ulfat interview, transcript by Mahin Vahdat, p. 1.
54 The three-year-old was probably Ahmad, Khadíjih's son.

evil actions and were frightened. I sat them next to me and soothed and consoled them. I had no news of my twenty-year-old son Áqá Mírzá 'Alí, of where he was or whether he had been killed by these evil people or was still alive. Nor did I know what had happened to my relatives who lived in that quarter. I was thinking of my children and my son-in-law. With the utmost fear, sadness and distress, I sat in a corner [of the garden] of Áqá Javád with my family around me, big and small. These children, who had at all times experienced only love and bounty and had had whatever they wanted, were now sitting next to me hungry and complaining of their hunger and I had no carpet [to sit on], no light, no bread, no water, nothing.

The people of that house, who were all my kith and kin and had always shown the utmost love and friendship towards us, were now all, both men and women, sitting at a distance from us, watching us and staying away from us. The men were dancing, clapping, singing and saying unseemly things. Sometimes they would go out of the house, sometimes they would come in in a state of merriment. One of them said, tomorrow, according to the orders of the clerics and of Há'irí, they will arrest the women of this religion and take them to the bazaar. They will parade them around the town and then take them to the clerics. Those of them who say they are Muslims and are prepared to curse [the Bahá'í Faith and its leaders] will be married off to Muslims. Those who do not curse and are 'Bábís' will be killed and [their bodies] burned. Another of them was singing and clapping and saying unseemly things and was expressing his joy and delight at our misfortune and grief. Another of them said that the news had just arrived that Áqá Muhammad Husayn 'Attár and his son had been found in such-and-such a house and had been killed. Instead of sympathizing with us and caring for us, they were rejoicing at our misfortune. [55]

Khadíjih Ulfat, who was the eldest child, aged 26 at this time, has given more details of how the episode began on 13 June 1903:

> It was 17 days after the month of Safar [i.e. 17th Rabí' al-Awwal]. It was the 'Id-i Mawlúd, the celebration of the birth of the Prophet [Muhammad]. In the houses they were chanting the Mawlúdí [religious poetry chanted on this occasion]. They had invited us. There were seven courtyards connected to each other. My sister (the mother of Dr Ulfat), my mother and I went together to the courtyard of my aunt [father's sister] for the Mawlúdí. They had brought an *akhúnd* (cleric) to chant the Mawlúdí. Eventually, my cousin, my father, his son-in-law (Mírzá Ibrahím) and my older brother finished their food and tea and went out of the door of the house. For no-one had heard yet [of the upheaval].
>
> Later, my cousin had been coming along the road and had seen a large crowd who had made flags and had gone to the house of Áqá Muhammad Ridá (whom they later martyred). They had poured into the house and were wrecking it and carrying off things. "Now they have come out again and are coming towards your house." He grasped my mother's hand and said: "Auntie (*zan dá'í*)! My dear auntie! Where is Mírzá 'Alí (her son)? They are coming towards your house." She replied: "I do not know. They have gone out."
>
> Looking through the connecting door, I saw that from the street, standing on another's shoulders, someone had climbed onto the roof and was shouting. Then everyone poured into our house. They knocked

---

55 Baydá, *Táríkh-i Baydá*, pp. 168-9.

everything about and then began to smash all of the glassware and break the doors. Then they pulled up our grape-vines and our pomegranate tree and our rose-bushes – whatever there was. They went into our cellar. Bottles of vinegar and of *áb-ghúrih* (juice of unripe grapes), bowls of yoghurt, and whatever else we had in our cellar, they smashed onto the ground and then they went smashing anything they came across as they went . . .

While they were smashing up the house, my cousin (*pisár-'ammih*) came out and said to them: "Destroy this place. This is the place where my uncle prays. Destroy this place." And they destroyed it.[56]

They went on to another house. Wherever they knew [was the home of a Bahá'í] they went there and if they did not know [of a Bahá'í house], the neighbours would say: "That is the house of a Bábí." And they would go to that house and wreck it and go on . . .

So anyway it was now night and the people had gone. Then we heard a banging of a pickaxe, they were pulling out the door of our yard. Our yard door was sturdy. We were in the courtyard belonging to my husband, we had gone there. Now they had taken up some pickaxes and in the dark night were hacking away. There were two or three of them breaking up the frame of the door. They had pulled out the two halves of the door. One of them took one half, one took the other and one of them took the door-frame.

Two or three hours of the night had passed and they continued to bang on our door. We went into our house. Our courtyard was large and I threw a carpet onto the ground in one corner of the yard. My mother,

---

56 Khadíjih Ulfat actually said this paragraph a little later in her narration but I have placed it here as this is where it should logically be.

Labíb (who was 10 years old), my sister [Vadí'ih] (who was 12 years old), [my son Jalál] Ulfat (who was 9 years old) and myself. There was no-one to give the children any food and they were hungry. On the other side of the yard, there was a pool and by it, my cousin [Áqá Ridá] and my husband's nephew [Áqá Javád] had fired up a samovar and were smoking a *qalyán* (hubble-bubble) They were saying: "Where is 'Abbás Effendi ['Abdu'l-Bahá] to come and defend them? Why does he not come to defend them? Ha! Ha! Ha!" They were laughing. And we were sitting over here in the dark without anyone and hungry.[57]

There was one person, a lady who was the grandmother of my husband, who had been saying her prayers in her room and had not joined the others [in the yard]. She came out and saw that, in one corner of the courtyard, they were sitting around, drinking tea smoking the *qalyán* and laughing and here we were sitting huddled around each other in the darkness. She started crying and said to me: "May I be a sacrifice for the Holy Family [*bimíram bará-yi ahl-i bayt* – the reference is to the family of the Iman Husayn after his martyrdom at Karbala]." From the other side of the courtyard, someone called out: "Dá'í Khatún, Dá'i Khátún (the wife of one's maternal uncle was called Dá'í Khatún). Are you comparing these people with those [the Holy Family]? They could not even compare

---

57 Khadíjih Ulfat later gives an account of what happened to this Áqá Javád. After she had moved to Tehran, she heard that the father and mother of Áqá Javád had died. After this he had gradually sold everything he had to survive. Eventually he had nothing left. He tried to go to Khurasan with a caravan but had to return as he was too hungry. He knocked on the door of his home, entered and fell down dead. His wife and children were left penniless. Eventually they went off to Khurasan where she had family. Khadíjih Ulfat interview, transcript by Mahin Vahdat, p. 23.

to the discarded nails of those [Holy Persons]. They are not even worthy to be the dust on the soles of their feet. It seems there is something wrong with you." She replied: "I came out and saw the children and these here and my heart was touched and so I said this. There is nothing wrong with me." She did not say anything more. She went and washed her hands. Then she went into her room saying "I have some bread and cheese." She brought these out and made them into portions and gave them to the children. They were crying because they were hungry. Their heads were in my lap. She gave each one of them a portion. They ate it and then they slept there until morning. We remained awake, sitting up. Three o'clock passed, five o'clock passed. What were we going to do?[58]

The events of that night are also recorded in Malmírí's history:

A large crowd of evily-disposed people who were mostly from the Malmír, Fahhádán, Kúshkanú, Bazár-i Naw and other nearby quarters of the town came with sticks, clubs, chains, rifles, swords, and stones – some had weighted scales and broken door frames. In this state, they came to the door of the house of Áqá Muhammad Husayn 'Attár, where they had been two or three times before and they had already burnt the door. This time they completely destroyed the door of the house and poured into the house. His respected wife was in the house with their sons and daughters, some young and some grown up, all except Áqá 'Alí, his eldest son.

As soon as the sound of the hullabaloo at the door

---

58 Khadíjih Ulfat interview, transcript by Mahin Vahdat, pp. 2-5.

of the house was heard, they fled through a connecting door to their neighbour, Áqá Javád 'Attár, for they were closely related, but the latter family were not inclined to give them refuge in their house. Their manner was one of being completely unconcerned about these people. So those poor people had to sit in a corner, silent and resigned to what was going on. The evil mob was busy wrecking and pilfering, breaking and spilling, burning and destroying. In the course of two hours, nothing was left that was worth even 100 dinars. They even pulled bricks off the house and carried them away. Suddenly they turned towards the house of Áqá Javád 'Attár and broke down the connecting door so that they could get in. Áqá Javád began to shout and swear at them and would not let anyone in.[59]

This account by Malmírí needs to be corrected by the previous account by Khadíjih Ulfat, who was an eye-witness. For example, it is clear that when the mob arrived, Fátimih-Sughrá had already gone to the house of their relative and neighbour Áqá Javád, having been invited to attend the celebrations of the Prophet's birth.

Frightening as that day had been, the next day was to bring even greater terrors for Fátimih-Sughrá. She woke that morning of 14 June 1903 in the courtyard of her wrecked house, with nothing to give her children for food, no money or possessions to obtain anything, not knowing whether her husband and older son were dead or alive. With much trepidation she decided to leave the house before dawn and find some food. She went first to the house of a Bahá'í neighbour Sayyid Abu'l-Qásim. She found out that he had faced down the mob and they

---

59 Malmírí, *Táríkh Shuhadá-yi Yazd*, pp. 177-8.

had not entered his house. But they had fled in the middle of the night so there was no help to be had from them. She decided to head for the Vaqt-u-Sá'at quarter where her daughter Sakinih lived. Her daughter Khadíjih Ulfat recalled the events of that day:

> When morning came, my mother, God bless her, said: "The children are hungry and our house is like this." She decided to go to the house of her son-in-law (the father of Dr Ulfat [Hájí Mírzá Ibráhím, the husband of Sakínih]). There they had a cloth-weaving factory. When she went there, she found at home his [Hájí Mírzá Ibráhím's] mother, an old lady, bent double (just like I am now), and there was no-one else there. Everyone else was hiding, they had gone away and were not around. So she went to that old lady and said the children and thus-and-so, they are hungry. Please give us from the factory some bread, cucumber, fresh herbs, and whatever else there is, so the children can eat.[60]

Fátimih-Sughrá thus managed to obtain some food and returned to her house. A short time later, however, the mob returned looking for her. Fatimih Sughra related her story thus to Baydá:

---

60 Khadíjih Ulfat interview, transcript by Mahin Vahdat, p. 5. The account in *Taríkh-i Baydá* (p. 171) is a little different. It says that Fátimih-Sughrá went to the Vaqt-u-Sa'át and it was Áqá Sayyidí, a relative of her son-in-law (Hájí Mírzá-yi Dámád), rather than her son-in-law's mother, who gave her some food and money and told that her daughter, son-in-law and other members of the family had gone into hiding the previous day and spent the time in a ditch of water.

A crowd came towards the house. They were saying my name and and asking where I was. I realized that they were after this poor wretched creature. I said to Javád-i 'Attár: "Áqá Javád! Say to them that she is not here and I will stand with these five or six women and they will not recognize me." But that accursed Javád pointed towards me and said: "Get out of this house. They are going to destroy us on account of you." So he showed me me over to that evil and foul crowd. Three of them were close to me. One of these was Javád the porter who lived in our quarter. Shamelessly and wickedly, he came towards me, grasped my hand and pulled me. They dragged me out of the house with the cotton cloak (*chádor*) that I had on in the house.

Outside, a crowd of about a hundred were gathered. They formed a procession and pushed me to the head of it. "We must go to the house of Navváb Vakíl. There she must either recant or we will kill her" they said. They pulled my cloak (*chádor*) from my head and, bare-headed and bare-footed, they made me walk the streets. Some fifty of them had knives, daggers or guns. Pointing at me, one of them would say: "I will strike her." Another said: "I will kill her." All I could do was turn to the Lord of the Worlds for I had no hope of escaping death. I feared that after killing me they would cut me up and hand out parts of me to these strangers in the streets and the bazaar.

Some fifty yards from the house, we reached a place where I could see in the distance Navváb Vakíl and a crowd who were standing there watching. As soon as they saw Navváb Vakíl, the crowd began to assault me. They grabbed my hair and started to pull me in different directions with it. One man who is a brocade-weaver (*sha'rbáf*) and whose name I have forgotten but he is the brother of Hájí 'Alí Maybudí punched me in the head, which made me go dizzy. He hit me so hard that he clasped his right hand, with which he had hit me, with his left hand and was saying: "Oh dear, my hand!" He had hurt his hand and up to now, which is eleven months later, his hand is still hurting, whatever the doctors, European or otherwise, have given him to rub into it. . . . They say that apart from this man who hit me in the head, a hundred others also hit me and a large crowd of others stood by and watched. Among them was the son of Hájí Muhammad Báqir Larí, whom I saw standing there with a handkerchief held to his mouth, laughing.

The crowd wanted to kill me. No-one was saying anything [to stop them] nor was anyone expressing any sympathy.[61]

Khadíjih Ulfat recalls:

My mother had managed to get some bread and cheese and cucumber and the apprentices of the factory brought them for us – it was some two quarters and two streets distant from us. No sooner had they put down these things than they [the mob] found out that the person [Fátimih-Sughrá] who had been away was now back. The same women who had been friends of my mother and who had been to our house, now came with scissors and knives in their hands. The men carried knives and other weapons. A large crowd poured into the house.

My mother said to these neighbours [i.e. Áqá Javád and his family who were relatives]: "If we all have our *chádor* [a piece of clothe that covers the body from head to foot and could be held across the face] on, they will go on to another house. Do not show me to them. Say that I have not come." One young girl, 14 or 15 years old, who had just been married said:

---

61 Baydá, *Tárikh-i Baydá*, pp. 172-74.

"Get away with you? Why should we say that you have not come? Curse [the Bahá'í Faith]! Curse [the Bahá'í Faith]!" And so my mother said: "I will go." [As she came out] They came forward and grasped my mother's hand and pulled her out into the street.

One person was saying: "My wife will cut off her hair with scissors." Another said: "We will cut off her head with a knife." In brief, her head-dress was pulled off her head. She told us: "I held my hands up over my face. The people just kept coming and hitting me. They dragged me to the end of the street." Muhammad the gun-powder maker (*barút-kúb*) arrived. He was a darvish and had a mantle over his shoulders. He took this off and threw it over my mother, whom he recognised, so that she would not be bare.

Some people went and told Navváb that this is the wife of Muhammad Husayn Bábí, whom they have dragged from her house and a crowd are taking her off. Navváb puts on his clothes, saying: "In what previous age has such a thing happened? Such a thing should only be done to a man. Why have they done it to a woman? Go quickly and prevent this. Take her to the house of the *kad-khudá* [headman of a city quarter]. Do not let them hurt this woman. Do not let them take her off." And so they took my mother off to the house of Ghulám-Husayn the *kad-khudá* and there they put her into a cellar underground. In this cellar, they were digging a well. Bare and beaten, with her body covered in bruises, she sat down. The wife of the *kad-khudá* told the people to go away.[62]

It can be seen that in this account, Khadíjih Khanum absolves Navváb Vakíl of blame in the episode but the

---

62 Khadíjih Ulfat interview, transcript by Mahin Vahdat, pp. 6-7.

previous account, which is from the words of Fatimih-Sughrá herself, says that Navváb Vakíl stood by, watching and lauging, and is more likely to be correct. In his history, Malmírí has obtained some of his information from Baydá's history, but he adds some other details:

> The evil that befell the respected wife of Áqá Muhammad Husayn 'Attár is very moving. On the previous day, which was a Friday, they had looted and destroyed their home. She had spent the night with her children in the house of Javád the pharmacist, who was a near relative. They spent that night without food and helpless. In the morning she put on her head-scarf and went off to the Vaqt-u-Sá'at quarter where there was a certain Sayyid, with whom she had family ties. She obtained a small sum from him with which she purchased some bread and cheese and returned to the house of Javád.
> They were just eating when the sound of a great hullabaloo arose nearby. They did not think that the crowd would go into a wrecked building. But suddenly they poured into the wrecked house and came to the door between the two houses. A few managed to get into the house of Javád looking for the wife of Áqá Muhammad Husayn. That good lady was standing with several other women. She said: "Say she is not here." But Javád, as well as saying: "She is not here", turned to that good lady and said: "Get out of my house, you. They are going to wreck my house on your account." Those evil persons, from the words and displeasure of Javád realised that this is the wife of that pure soul. A certain Javád, who was a porter in that same Fahhádán quarter came forward and grasped the hand of that poor lady and took her out of the house with that same silk prayer head-dress that she had on.

There were about a hundred people in the street and in that vicinity standing, crowding one behind the other. The children ran out after their poor mother. Suddenly they formed a procession [*shahí*] with that respected lady at the head of it, saying that they must take her to the of the Navváb Vakíl. "If she curses [Bahá'u'lláh], we will let her go; if she does not, we will kill her." This crowd were so crazed and were creating such an uproar – one person was gesticulating with a dagger and chanting, another was brandishing a knife, another had drawn a revolver – that, minute by minute, the crowd was increasing and the street was filling up with men and women, most of them just watching. With this procession [*sháh vaqiyyih*] and hullabaloo, they brought that poor lady to their destination in the Fahhádán quarter. The Nawwab Vakil and his brothers came out just to watch. They joined the crowd. Several people began to beat that virtuous lady so much with their hands and with sticks that she became weak. Suddenly, they pulled the *chádor* off that pure and blameless young woman and tore apart her *chárqad* [head-dress]. They wound her hair around their hands and kept beating her. They intended to kill her. All these people were watching and were joyful and laughing and no-one asked why they were doing this.

Muhammad the gunpowder maker (*barút-kúb*) who is now a pharmacist and is wealthy and a believer – although, since he has wealth, he is afraid to associate with the believers and come to their meetings – used to wear darvish clothes, because that was a safe set of clothes to wear – most of the darvishes are irreligious and unrestrained and so people do not engage them in conversation or have dealings with them. He had a ferocious voice and he turned to Javád the pharmacist and said: "Javád 'Attar, woe to you! I spit on you! You unmanly and dishonourable coward! Why have you let this poor, respectable woman fall into the hands of this irreligious, evil and ungodly mob, that they have done this to her." Then with his fearsome voice, he turned to the crowd and roared: "O you irreligious people! What is happening? What religion do you have? If you be Muslims, then it is forbidden to you in religious law to be in the presence of this lady (*ná-mahrám*). Why have you pulled her head-dress off and uncovered her hair? What sort of religion is this that you have? May God curse you irreligious people that you stand there gleefully watching someone's wife which you are forbidden to do in religious law. Go away you irreligious wretches." He pulled the poor woman over and took a *chádor* that Javád's wife had sent after her and threw it over her head. Then he turned towards Nawwáb Vakíl and said: "O Navváb, you say that you keep order in the town. It is a strange sort of order you are keeping. You have come to watch! Why are you not holding back this mob?"

Indeed God gave such a power and strength to Áqá Muhammad that it is a source of wonder. The Nawwáb was embarrassed and said: "It is not my responsibility. Hand her over to Ghulám-Husayn the *kad-khudá* so that he may safely take her to the house of the Imám-Jum'ih. The decision in this matter rests with the Imám-Jum'ih. Mírzá Muhammad, the son of Hájí Mírzá Hasan Shaykhí, very much wanted to harm or kill that poor woman. They handed her over to Ghulám-Husayn, the *kad-khudá* of that same Fahhádán quarter, in order that he might take her to the house of the Imám-Jum'ih. Then, whatever the Imám-Jum'ih decided, they would carry it out. He took that respected lady and walked her to his house and imprisoned her in his cellar. He said to her: "Give me ten *túmáns* and I will help you and put matters right for you."

That poor lady [the wife of Áqá Muhammad Husayn] called out from her prison for the wife of Ghulám-Husayn. The sister of Ghulám-Husayn came and that poor lady entreated her saying: "I am not afraid of being killed, but I am afraid that they may strip me naked and drag me through the streets and bazaars in front of strangers." She had some gold earrings on her ears and she took them off and gave them to the sister of Ghulám-Husayn and said: "These are worth twenty túmáns. Give them to Ghulám-Husayn to free me from this house."

Meanwhile the children of that poor lady were wandering the streets covered in dust and blood and no-one had gathered these children and comforted them.[63]

The accounts of what happened after this, differ somewhat in detail. Malmírí seems to indicate that Fátimih-Sughrá did not spend long in the cellar of the house of *kád-khudá* before being rescued by her relative Mulla Husayn, who took her to the Imám-Jum'ih and there obtained a judgement that she was innocent of any wrong-doing. Khadíjih Ulfat states that Fátimih-Sughra was in the cellar for three days. Since Khadíjih Ulfat would have had to be responsible for the welfare of her brothers and sisters during this time, it is likely that her account is more accurate.[64]

At the house of *kad-khudá,* they told my mother: "We will not give you anything to eat." Later when the wife of the *kad-khuda* came down, [my mother] said: "Please give me some water to drink. I am dying of

---

63 Malmírí, *Táríkh Shuhadá-yi Yazd*, pp. 267-271.
64 Muhammad Labib confirms that it was 3 days in *Khatirát-i Shast Rúzih*, manuscript, p. 6.

thirst." She said: "Oh really! You bastard Bábí. Are you wheedling up to me? You want some water?" And then she turned to her daughter and said: "Go and urinate in a water-melon skin and bring it for her to drink." And so they did not give her any water to drink. My mother was in the house of the kad-khudá. The wife of the *kad-khudá* then said: "Tell me about whatever you have, so I can go and get it." My mother replied: "By God! Whatever there was in the house, the people have taken away. I have nothing else" . . .

After three days, a certain Áqá Hasan Tarráz (embroiderer), who was a master cloth-weaver and Hájí Mírzá ['Alí, husband of Khadíjih Ulfat] was his apprentice, said: "It has been three days that they have taken that poor woman and no-one has been to see her. Come with me to the house of Ghulám-Husayn [the *kad-khudá*]." [Hájí Mírzá 'Alí] said: "I am ready to come with you." Together they went there and saw that she was in the cellar. She said to them: "It is three days that I have tasted nothing except fear. Now that you have come, please get me a bowl of cool water with some sugar dissolved in it to drink. They returned home and, with Áqá Hasan Tarráz, prepared some sugar dissolved in water and took it.

We had a relative [who was *mu'adhdhin*, the person who calls people to prayers][65] – Mullá Husayn. He was a relative of my father. He did not know of what had happened. Then someone came to him and told

---

65 At this point Khadíjih Ulfat makes an aside about the minaret of the Jum'ih Mosque in Yazd: "You have not seen Yazd. The Jum'ih Mosque there has a tall minaret with many steps going up. At the top is the balcony (*gul-dastih*), from which the call to prayer is made. In the whole town, its sound is heard. In the month of Ramadan, they recite the *Rawdih* (recital of the sufferings of Imám Husayn) from there, as well as prayers, dawn prayers and so on."

him that they had taken the wife of that man Husayn who is your uncle (*dá'í*) to the house of the *kad-khudá*. He said: "Why did you not inform me of this earlier?" He went [to the house of the *kad-khudá*] and asked: "Why have you brought this woman here?" Then he went down into the cellar and said to my mother: "Get up, we are going. Who dares say anything to me?" She said: "My head is uncovered. I have nothing. Please get me a black *chádor* or something." He went and found a *cháqshúr* (hose). When he had found one, he came and gave it to my mother and said: "Put this on and come with me. Who dares to say yea or nay?" My mother put it on and came out of the house of the *kad-khudá*. He [Mullá Husayn] was saying: "Why did you not inform me sooner? Why have you only told me now? Why have to kept her here? Why have you allowed them to take her?" And they went.[66]

It appears that Mullá Husayn took Fatimih-Sughrá back to her house. But she was so unwell that she could not stay there. Khadíjih Ulfat continues:

Someone came and took my mother. When they were out of the house, she asked: "Where are we going?" "To the Shirází's [Afnán's] house." And they went. By the time they got there, my mother was almost dead. They put down some bedding and laid her down. Then the women came with medicines (*múmiyá'í*) and oil. They put this on their hands and rubbed it all over her body. For several days, perhaps a week, they continued to rub her in this way and massage her. All her body was covered in bruises. After a week, they came and took her to the baths and put clothes on her. They kept

---

66 Khadíjih Ulfat interview, transcript by Mahin Vahdat, pp. 7-8

FÁTIMIH-SUGHRÁ 59

her there [at the Afnán's house] for some time.

Later, when the people had been restrained somewhat and had collected themselves a little, then my mother came home . . . But our home was a ruin, so we gathered at the house of her son-in-law – the father of Dr Ulfat [i.e. the house of her daughter Sakínih and Hájí Mírzá Ibráhím] – in the Vaqt-u-Sá'at quarter.[67]

Eventually, as recorded in the story of Áqá Muhammad Husayn, her husband return from Bavánát and there was a joyous reunion of husband and wife at the Afnán's house. As described above, Áqá Muhammad Husayn then had a period of ill-health, through which Fátimih-Sughrá nursed him. It was then necessary to contemplate their future. The fact that Fátimih-Sughrá had been publicly undressed and humiliated was a major factor in their considerations. It is difficult for anyone without experience of the conditions of an intensely conservative and traditional society such as that of Yazd to understand the enormity of what had occurred. As in all traditional societies, the social role of the women was closely controlled and their freedoms severely limited. As a result of their interpretation of religious law, one major social taboo that was that it was not permissible for any man to talk to or to see the face or any part of the body of a mature woman to whom he was not either married or very closely related. To appear in public without the

---

67 Khadíjih Ulfat interview, transcript by Mahin Vahdat, pp. 8-9. At this point Khadíjih Ulfat makes an aside which appears to be about the Vaqt-u-Sá'at quarter saying: "There at 'Áshúrá [commemoration of the martyrdom of Imám Husayn on 10th Muharram], they carry around a *naql* [usually a model of the shrine of Imám Husayn] in procession."

chádor (a piece of cloth that covered the body from head to foot and could be held across the face) would be tantamount to appearing naked, it would imply a complete lack of morals. Only a woman of disreputable character, of loose morals, a prostitute, would appear in this way – and in the normal course of things no woman would dare to try because she would be attacked. The fact that Fátimih-Sughrá's appearance in a public place without her *chádor* had not been voluntary and that indeed she had been dragged out into the street and her chádor had been ripped away was not a sufficient defence in the eyes of the people. In common with most traditional patriarchal societies, women get the blame for the crimes committed against them by men. The victim is turned into the accused. Thus for example, a woman who is raped is accused of having brought it upon herself and of having tempted the man beyond his ability to resist. Thus Fátimih-Sughrá knew that although she was completely blameless, she would have to spend the rest of her life being considered a disreputable woman in that fiercely conservative and unforgiving society.

Malmírí in trying to explain the enormity of the situation that faced Áqá Muhammad Husayn and Fátimih-Sugrá writes:

> That disaster that had befall his [Áqá Muhammad Husayn's] respected wife has not befallen anyone else. Indeed, martyrdom would have been easier to bear than the malicious gloating and the dishonouring of one's reputation. The question of the veiling of women was one that was held to be of great importance in Yazd. So much so that if the *rawdih-kháns* (reciters of the tragedy of martyrdom of the Imám Husayn) had said

that the Holy Family, after the events in the desert of Karbalá and as they were being brought captive to Damascus, had been without veils, most of the people would have objected to this statement [even though it is what happened]. They would have said that it is a lie; how could the family and wives of Imám Husayn be without veils. And now the shamelessness of this mob had reached such a stage that they had removed not just the *chádor* but also the head-scarf from this respectable lady and had dragged her, with her hair uncovered, all bloodied and covered with dirt, through the streets. The shame of this disgraceful deed and the imprisonment in the house of the kad-khudá was greater than martyrdom.[68]

A while later, 'Abdu'l-Bahá wrote tablets in which he comforts Fátimih-Sughrá for the shame and violation that she had endured. One tablet of 'Abdu'l-Bahá is addressed to Fátimih-Sughrá and her children, but the main import of his words are to Fátimih-Sughrá herself. In his tablet, 'Abdu'l-Bahá refers to the indignities that she had suffered. The following is a provisional translation:

> To the maid-servant of God the wife of Áqá Husayn 'Attár and her sons, Mírzá 'Alí Muhammad and Mírzá Muhammad Mihdí and her daughters, the maid-servant of God Khadíjih, the maid-servant of God Raqiyyih, and the maid-servant of God Sakínih, upon them all be the Glory of God, the Most Glorious.

---

68 Malmírí, *Khátirát-i-Malamírí*, p. 102.

He is God!

O ye oppressed ones! Be not sorrowful, neither be ye grieved or dismayed. Although your hearts and souls were the targets of spears and arrows, yet it was for the sake of the Friend and on the pathway of the Beloved.

> If He should confer upon thee a pearl,
>   its shell should be thy heart
> And should arrows of hardship come thy way,
>   their target should be thy soul.

Although your house and home have been laid waste, yet praised be to God, in the Divine rose-garden, upon the tree of Tubá, ye have a nest waiting and prepared for you. The fate of buildings made of earth is eventually to be flattened and the pleasures of this ephemeral world become grief and disappointment. How much better is it, therefore, that such weak houses be shed from our load in the pathway of the undying Lord, so that a mighty palace might be erected in a new Kingdom. So therefore, whatever blows fell upon your person are indeed a bounty and bare-headedness is the highest degree of chastity and purity. What could be better than that a human being should, in the pathway of the Beloved, meet with the utmost disdain and encounter disgrace in the world? The result of this is indeed Divine favour and eternal glory in the world of Mercy. Praise be to God that you do not complain, but rather you are thankful.

Upon ye be greetings and praise. 'Ayn 'Ayn.[69]

---

69 Muhammad Labib, *Khatirát-i Shast Rúzih*, manuscript, p. 7, 8. Malmírí, *Khátirát-i-Malamírí*, p. 103. The verse quoted is from Sana'i Ghaznavi, Qasídih no. 15.

Muhammad Labib explains the meaning of this tablet thus:

> Because the mob fell upon our house and pulled cloak (*chádor*) off my mother's head and winding her long hair around their hands they had dragged my mother along the ground in the streets in front of a large crowd. After tormenting her and torturing her in innumerable ways and injuring her and cutting her with knifes, whips, sticks and stones, they took her off to the prison. It is for this reason that 'Abdu'l-Bahá refers to her bare-headedness in this tablet.[70]

Because of their impossible situation, Áqá Muhammad Husayn decided to move to Tehran. He left for that city in order to find work and a house, leaving behind Fátimih-Sughrá in Yazd, to try to look after the children despite her difficult situation. Three years later, in 1906, he sent for his wife and family. Leaving behind her two married daughters, Fátimih-Sughrá set off on the long journey to Tehran.

Muhammad Labib describes that journey to Tehran thus:

> We were on this journey, which is about 700 kilometres, for about 33 days on mules and asses. Because the road was not safe we travelled with a group of others who were not Bahá'ís. The grooms who were guiding this caravan were bigoted Muslims. They realised that we were Bahá'ís and ill-treated and harassed us the whole way.[71]

---

70 Muhammad Labib, *Khatirát-i Shast Rúzih*, manuscript, p. 12.
71 Muhammad Labib, *Khatirát-i Shast Rúzih*, manuscript, p. 12.

In Tehran, the family settled down and tried to re-create a life for themselves. While her husband began to work in order to bring in an income, Fatimih-Sughrá continued the difficult task of raising their children despite their straitened circumstances. When her daughter Sakínih died in about 1921, 'Abdu'l-Bahá consoled Fatima-Sughrá with these words:

> Haifa, 5/10/21
> Through Hájí Amín,
> To the Maid-servant of God, the wife of Áqá Muhammad Husayn 'Attár Yazdí
>
> O Servant of the Lord! Be assured of the bounties and grace of the One True God. Thy daughter hath taken her flight unto the Heaven of Forgiveness. Well is it with her! Happy is she! Thou art not alone. God is with thee. Thou art under the shelter of the favour of Blessed Perfection.[72]

From all reports, Fátimih-Sughrá never really recovered from her ordeal in Yazd. She remained unwell for the rest of her life. She developed a condition of the heart and was frequently ill and sometimes fainted. Despite these maladies, she lived on until her death a short time after her husband in 1936.

---

72 From typed copy of tablet in possession of Mahin Vahdat.

Prayer and Tablet of 'Abdu'l-Bahá for the Family

Among the most precious items that belong to the family is a prayer revealed by 'Abdu'l-Bahá for the family. The story of the revelation of this prayer is as follows. At the Tímchih-yi Hájibu'd-Dawlih, the small caravansarai in Tehran where Áqá Muhammad Husayn had his pharmacy, there were also a number of Zoroastrian-born Bahá'ís who owned a company called Parsiyán. Several of them decided to visit 'Abdu'l-Bahá and as was customary among Bahá'ís, numerous Bahá'í gave them petitions to take to 'Abdu'l-Bahá. It was a common practice among Bahá'ís to send a petition requesting 'Abdu'l-Bahá's prayers and confirmations. Muhammad Labíb writes:

> The head of the company, Áqá Arbáb Shahriyár, was a close friend of Áqá Muhammad Husayn. He stated that many of the Bahá'ís had written petitions to 'Abdu'l-Bahá and it was timely that Áqá Muhammad Husayn should do likewise. It should be mentioned that my father, from the first moment that he declared as a Bahá'í, never wished to be a trouble to the Blessed Perfection Bahá'u'lláh, nor would he present petitions to 'Abdu'l-Bahá. Nevertheless several holy tablets from Bahá'u'lláh and some from 'Abdu'l-Bahá in his own hand were graciously and bounteously revealed for him without his presenting a request. Some of these tablets were as a result of the favourable mention that was made of his name by some of the pilgrims, and this

would result in the revelation of a tablet.

'Abdu'l-Bahá was very kind and gracious towards my father and wrote several tablets in his own hand to him, which contained important matters. But at the time when this group of pilgrims were going and, at their insistence, he willy-nilly copied the custom of the other Bahá'ís and wrote a short petition to be presented to 'Abdu'l-Bahá. Arbáb Shahriyár who was the head of this group of Zoroastrian-born pilgrims and had taken with him the petition of my father, described what happened:

At around the time of sunset, this group of pilgrims met with 'Abdu'l-Bahá, each one of them brought forward the bundles of petitions that they had brought from the Bahá'ís, each of which was wrapped in a silk handkerchief. We placed them on a table in the room and then sat down. 'Abdu'l-Bahá rose from his seat and stretched forward and picked one of these petitions up. It was fate that it was the short petition of my father. On the margin of the petition, in his own hand, he wrote a prayer in honour of this family.[73]

The text of the petition from Áqá Muhammad Husayn was as follows (see photographs at the end of the book):

O 'Abdu'l-Bahá! May my soul and my reality be a sacrifice for the dust of the footsteps of thy Friends. All are thirsty for the water of your bounty. Be merciful unto us.

This evanescent one Husayn 'AT,
His wife, Fátimih-Sughra
My son, 'Ali Muhammad
the other, Muhammad Mahdi [Labíb]
my daughter, Khadíjih

---

73 Muhammad Labib, *Khatirát-i Shast Rúzih*, manuscript, p. 10.

the other, Sakínih
the other, Ruqiyyih [Vadí'ih]
my grand-son, Jalál
the other, Amínu'lláh
the other, Ahmad 'Alí

We are in need of your grace.

'Abdu'l-Bahá has written across the top of the sheet a prayer of which the following is a provisional translation:

> O Educator of all creation! These souls are submitting unto Thee and, with the utmost humility, are looking towards Thy kingdom. Therefore the hope of this Servant of Thy threshold is this: that Thou mayest be their shelter and their refuge. 'Ayn 'Ayn.[74]

> *Ay morabbí-yi vojúd, ín nufús ahl-i sojúd-and va dar naháyat-i tazzaro' beh malakút shahúd. Laházá, rejá-yi ín bandeh-yi dargáh án-ast keh ánán rá malja' va panáh báshí. 'Ayn 'Ayn.*[75]

In a tablet of 'Abdu'l-Bahá addressed to Muhammad Labíb while he was on pilgrimage in 1919, many members of the family are addressed. Muhammad Labíb himself is mentioned first as the pilgrim who is present, then his parents Áqá Muhammad Husayn and Fátimih-

---

74 A facsimile of this petition and prayer is in Muhammad Labib, *Khatirát-i Shast Rúzih*, manuscript, p. 9 and is transcribed on p. 10.
75 I have tried to transliterate in a way that will be useful to anyone wanting to read the prayer. In the Bahá'í transliteration system, it would be: *Ay murabbí-yi vujúd, ín nufús ahl-i sujúd-and va dar naháyat-i taḍḍaru' bih malakút shahúd. Laháḍhá, rijá-yi ín bandih-yi dargáh án-ast kih ánán rá malja' va panáh báshí. 'Ayn 'Ayn.*

Sughrá, followed by their three sons-in-law, then their daughters, each being named individually together with their children:

> O pilgrim who art present and thy father Áqá Muhammad Husayn and mother Fátimih-Sughrá, their sons-in-law, Hájí Mírzá Ibráhím Nafahát, Hájí Mirzá 'Alí Khushhál, and Áqá Mírzá Muhammad Khán Mu'min, and their children, Bíbí Sakínih and Mírzá Amínu'lláh, Bíbí Khadíjih, Mírzá Jalál Ulfat, and Ahmad 'Alí, and the maid-servant of God Vadí'ih and her children Mahbúbih, 'Ishqu'lláh and Sidratu'lláh, and Mírza 'Alí!
>
> These souls have, one and all, drawn near to the court of the One True God and are attracted to the effulgences of the All-Merciful. They are subject to the glances of His Favour and are under the watchful gaze of the True One. Favoured are they and honoured. Exalted are they and illumined. Convey to them, each and every one, the most wondrous and most glorious greetings from me.[76]

---

76 Tablet sent to the Bahá'í World Centre by Muhammad Labib.

Khadíjih Ulfat

Khadíjih Ulfat was born in Yazd in about 1877, the eldest daughter of Áqá Muhammad Husayn and Fátimih-Sughrá. Khadíjih has told a story of something that happened when she was an infant:

> Because the weather in Yazd in the summer gets very hot, people would go out to the villages. I was two or three months old when they put me on a mule and set off. When the donkey wanted to jump over a stream, I fell into the water. Only the muleteer noticed that the baby had fallen into the water. He picked me up and gave me back to my mother with soaking wraps.[77]

Khadíjih was about five years of age when her father became a Bahá'í in about 1882. She was very conscious of the fact that she was a Bahá'í while she was growing up. She remembered that in about 1884, when she was about seven, her father was imprisoned and beaten because he was a Bahá'í (see story of Áqá Muhammad Husayn Ulfat). At the time of the 1891 persecutions that led to the Seven Martyrs of Yazd, when her father was again arrested and beaten, she was fourteen years of age.

She was only nine years of age when she was married to her first husband Áqá Mírzá Muhammad in about 1886. The story behind this marriage was that her father and Áqá Mírzá Muhammad had been close

---

77 Khadíjih U lfat interview, transcript by Mahin Vahdat, p. 20.

friends in their youth and had made an agreement that they would marry two sisters. When Áqá Muhammad Husayn married Fátimih-Sughrá and she had no sister, Áqá Mírzá Muhammad said that he would wait until they had a daughter and then marry her. And so it was that in fulfilment of this agreement, Khadíjih was married at the age of nine.

Khadíjih was about 17 when she had her first child Jalál in about 1894. She then had two more children, Qamar and Diyá (Ziyá) who died during infancy. Qamar was about one year of age when she died.

Khadíjih Ulfat recounted some of the routines of her family life at that time in Yazd. She recalled:

> When it was summer, those who were in the villages, such as Manshad and Bavánát would come to town, so that those who were in the town could go to the villages. Everyone would have a particular place that they would go to. My father would always go to Manshad. He had found a house-owner there called Áqá Sayyid Husayn. He had recently married. For three years consecutively we went to his house. It was also the time when I had just married. I was 11 or 12 years old.[78]

Her first husband must have died in about 1897 and Khadíjih married again shortly afterwards. Her second husband was Hájí Mírzá 'Alí. He was known in the family as Hájí Mírzá Kúchik – as distinct from the husband of Sakínih, who was Hájí Mirzá Buzurg (kúchik

---

78 Khadíjih Ulfat interview, transcript by Mahin Vahdat, p. 21. She goes on to state: "They killed Áqá Sayyid Husayn and one of his sons who was just 12 years old in that year (1903) and buried them there in his house because he was a Bahá'í."

means small or younger, *buzurg* means great or older). In around 1899, she had a son Ahmad. When in later years, surnames became compulsory, Áqá Muhammad Husayn said that the whole family should have the same surname, and so Hájí Mírzá 'Alí also adopted the surname Ulfat. He was a cloth-weaver and embroiderer. He was not a Bahá'í. Khadíjih lived with her husband and children in a house situated among a complex of houses in which other members of her father's family lived. She describes it thus:

> [It was in] Kúchih-yi Kitábkhánih (the road of the library) . . . Kuchih-yi Hájí 'Alí Mullá Zaynab. There were two brothers, one was Hájí 'Alí Mulla Zaynab and the other Hájí Muhammad Mullá Zaynab. They had black man-servants and woman-servants in their house. There would be *rawdih-khánís* (recitals of the sufferings of Husayn) at their house. They were very wealthy and had many things. Our house was in their road. The first house was theirs. Then you would go along the road which was narrow and it was a long way to the end. Each part of it was the house of someone else. The whole quarter was called the Yúzárún quarter. The house of Áqá Sultán[79] was in the Kúchih-yi Qadam-gáh. There was a *qadam-gáh* (an area for strolling) at the end of the road where my father's house was. There was also a bath (*hamám*). Steps went down to it, so they called it Hamám-i Gawdak (the *hamám* in a little hollow). The back of this bath faced onto our road. You would open a door and go in.[80]

---

79 This was a relative of Muhammad the gun-powder maker (*barút-kúb*), the dervish who saved Fátimih-sughrá. Their family name later wasNík-Á'yín.
80 Khadíjih Ulfat interview, transcript by Mahin Vahdat, p. 19.

Khadíjih also described the family house thus:

> The house of my father has lasted well. There were eight courtyards each of them had an opening to the other. Our house (Khadíjih and her husband's) had a large courtyard. There were also two cellars in our house, one at one end of the courtyard, which belonged to Áqá Javád (my husband's nephew) and the other at the other end, belonging to us. When you went into it in the summer to sleep, it was so cold that you had to put a matress down and to pull a blanket over you. There were three springs of water in the cellar. In the old days, they did not used to have doors. There was a ring and above was a lock to be shut. The guest-room was in the house.[81]

Khadíjih had clear memories of the 1903 upheaval against the Bahá'ís in Yazd. She was at this time 26 years old. Much of her role during this upheaval can be gleaned from the above account of what happened to her mother. Being the eldest daughter, she had to support her mother during a very difficult period. She was with her mother and siblings when news of the upheaval first came and she was present when the mob broke into their house and ransacked and looted it. The next day, she was left in charge of her children and siblings when her mother went off to try to find some food for them. She recalled how during her mother's absence, the mob returned:

> While she (my mother) was out, I suddenly saw a group of men coming to the door of the house, then they

---

[81] Khadíjih Ulfat interview, transcript by Mahin Vahdat, p. 24.

poured in. I with my sister (Ruqiyyih, later Vadí'ih), we two were sitting next to each other in front of a large window (*panj-darí*) with the children. Then we saw the men coming in through the door. They said: "Where has she gone?" I said: "She has gone out." They said: "Where has she gone to do?" I said: "You go and when she comes back, we will let you know."[82]

When Fátimih-Sughrá eventually returned with some food, the mob also returned and dragged her away. For three days, Khadíjih had to look after the children in a ruined house with no means at her disposal, not knowing what had happened to her mother and father. She recalls what happened during those three days as people returned time and again to ransack the house.

For three days, the doors of our house were open and people came and took away everything there was, doors, glasses, even the bricks. They took everything. Eventually after three days, the Navváb sent some men to fill in our yard gate with packed mud.[83]

During this time, Fátimih-Sughrá was in the cellar of Ghulám-Husayn, the *kad-khudá*. His wife tried to extort money from Fátimih-Sughrá. Although Fátimih-Sughrá tried to explain to her that she had nothing left, that her house had been completely ransacked, yet Khadíjih Ulfat remembers:

That day, I saw a fat lady with drooping breasts come to our house. She stood there at the gate of our house with

---

82 Khadíjih Ulfat interview, transcript by Mahin Vahdat, p. 5.
83 Khadíjih Ulfat interview, transcript by Mahin Vahdat, p. 7.

her head-dress on, saying: "Give me whatever your mother has." When I said: "By God! Lady, ask those people. Whatever there was in the house, they have taken." She did not say anything else and went away. [84]

After three days, Fátimih-Sughrá was brought back to the house, but as the house was ransacked and Fatimih-Sughrá was very ill as a result of her ordeals, she was taken off to the Afnán's house, and Khadíjih was again left to look after the children. Eventually, being unable to live in their ruined house, they moved to the house of her sister, Sakínih, and brother-in-law, Hájí Mírzá Ibrahím in the Vaqt-u-Sá'at quarter. Khadíjih remembers:

> . . . we and the children were all together in a small room about this size [4x3 metres].[85] When it became night, we would lay down the cushions and throw blankets over them. If anyone wanted to get up [in the middle of the night], it was necessary to carefully put one's foot between the feet of the others and so go out of the room.[86]

Even at this stage, Khadíjih recalls that they were not aware of what had happened to all of their family. Her brother 'Alí had disappeared on that first day of the persecution and there was no news of him.

> One day, there was a noise and someone came saying: "He was in the ditch (*júb*). I saw it myself. I saw it myself. At the pool in the public square (*hawd-i*

---

84 Khadíjih Ulfat interview, transcript by Mahin Vahdat, p. 7.
85 Khadíjih Ulfat was at this time sitting up in bed, in her bedroom which was about 4x3 metres.
86 Khadíjih Ulfat interview, transcript by Mahin Vahdat, p. 9.

KHADÍJIH ULFAT 75

maydán) – they cut off the head of 'Alí the Bábí there."
I said: "For God's sake, are you telling the truth?" [He said:] "By God! I saw it myself. I saw it with my own eyes. They cut off the head of 'Alí the Bábí by the pool in the public square."[87]

For two months there was no other news of 'Alí, until one day he emerged from the subterranean water-channels where he had been hiding and came to them in Sakínih's house in the Vaqt-u-Sá'at quarter. He was so altered that Khadíjih says that she did not recognise him.

When her mother and father left for Tehran after the 1903 episode, Khadíjih remained in Yazd for a time with her husband and children. After a few years in about 1908, Áqá Muhammad Husayn sent for her elder son Jalál to come to Tehran to go to the Tarbiyat school there.

Khadíjih Khanum's other son Ahmad Ulfat married Rubábih (Mihrangiz) Dargáhí. He worked for Sázmán-i Barnamih (Plan Organization). They had no children. He was stationed at Zanjan for a long time. He died before his mother and news of his death was kept from her as she was very elderly and died a few years later.

Eventually Khadíjih Khánum and her husband moved to Tehran. She remained there until 1935 when she moved with her husband to Kirman, where her son Jalál was working as the head of the customs. He had previously been *názim* (school superintendent) of the Bahá'í School in Hamadan, then head of customs in Abadan and had also been stationed in Qasr-i Shirin. They remained in Kerman until 1939. They then returned to Tehran, where they remained for the rest of their

---

87 Khadíjih Ulfat interview, transcript by Mahin Vahdat, p. 10.

lives. There he worked for a pharmaceutical wholesaler call Irántúr. He was active on Bahá'í committees, such as Lajnih-yi Huqúqí (reconciling Bahá'ís who were at loggerheads with each other). She and her husband, her son Jalal and her grand-daughter Rúhí lived in the house that had belonged to Áqá Muhammad Husayn.

Rúhí was married in 1949 to Sayyid Muhammad 'Ali Ghiassi Razavi, who worked for the Kishávarzí Bank (Agricultural Bank). He knew Rúhí's father and the marriage was arranged thus. Dr Varqá's wife is also from the same family as Mr Razaví. Their children were Riaz, Razi, Hami and Olia. Riaz and Razi were particularly famous for their naughtiness and tricks when they were small. In 1975, Riaz went to the Holy land and from there to Africa. He settled at first in Malawi, and then in Lesotho, where he became a member of the National Spiritual Assembly in 1979. In 1983, he moved to the African homeland of Ciskei in South Africa. He was the director of finance at the University of Fort Hare. On 13 March 1994, while attending a meeting at the Bahá'í Centre at Mdantsane, Ciskei, gunmen burst in the building and shot the three Iranians who were present in a racially motivated attack. One of these three who died was Riaz Razavi. The Universal House of Justice sent the following telegram:

> SHOCKED GRIEVED NEWS VIOLENT DEATH HOUSHMAND ANVARI, SHAMAM BAKHSHANDAGI AND REZA RAZAVI IN CISKEI. PROFOUNDLY IMPRESSED STERLING EXAMPLE SET BY THEIR DEDICATION CAUSE BAHÁ'U'LLÁH IN WHOSE SERVICE THEY WERE DIRECTLY ENGAGED WHEN STRUCK

DOWN BY ASSASSINS' BULLETS. DEEPLY SYMPATHIZE IRREPARABLE LOSS THEIR DEAR FAMILIES AND FRIENDS. MAY ALL HEARTS BE COMFORTED BY PROMISE BLESSED BEAUTY THAT THEY THAT HAVE FORSAKEN THEIR COUNTRY IN PATH GOD AND SUBSEQUENTLY ASCENDED UNTO HIS PRESENCE SHALL BE BLESSED BY CONCOURSE ON HIGH AND THEIR NAMES RECORDED BY PEN GLORY AMONG SUCH AS HAVE LAID DOWN THEIR LIVES AS MARTYRS PATH GOD. CONFIDENT JOYOUS WELCOME ABHÁ KINGDOM THESE DISTINGUISHED SOULS. ARDENTLY PRAYING HOLY SHRINES THEIR PROGRESS DIVINE WORLD.[88]

Khadíjih Khanum's husband died in 1964 and her son Jalál Ulfat died in 1965. She then moved in with her niece, Mahin Vahdat. To her sister Vadí'ih's family, she was always known as "Khálih Khánum" or "Khálih Jún". She died on 23 October 1977, at the age of 100 years.

---

88 *The Bahá'í World 1993-94* (Haifa: Bahá'í World Centre, 1994), pp. 149-50.

Sakínih Ulfat

Sakínih was the second surviving child of Áqá Muhammad Husayn and Fátimih-Sughrá and was born in Yazd. The date of her birth is uncertain. She married Hájí Mírzá Ibrahím, who owned a cloth-weaving factory in the Vaqt-u-Sá'at quarter (Maydán-i Shah and Mír Chaqmáq). She moved to his house there. Later when surnames became compulsory, he also took the name Ulfat at Áqá Muhammad Husayn's request. There was one son from that marriage, Dr Amínu'lláh Ulfat. He was born in about 1900.

When the upheaval of 1903 took place, Sakínih was already married and living in her husband's house, so she was not present when the family home was destroyed on 13 June 1903. She and her husband went into hiding, and so it was that when Fátimih-Sughrá came seeking help on the following day, there was only Hájí Mírzá Ibrahím's mother there.

After some days, with the house of Áqá Muhammad Husayn and Fátimih-Sughrá destroyed, Sakinih's parents and their children came and lived with them, until they moved to Tehran in about 1905. She and her husband moved to Tehran shortly afterwards and bought a house next to Áqá Muhammad Husayn Ulfat in Kúchih-yi Malik. Sakínih Khanum died young in early 1920. On her passing, 'Abdu'l-Bahá revealed a prayer to be said for her:

> O my God! O my God! This is Thy blessed servant Sakínih who hath hastened unto Thee and humbled herself at the threshold of Thy Mercy, imploring Thy pardon and forgiveness, earnestly seeking Thy Grace and Beneficence, entreating Thy Kingdom of Mercy, sincerely looking to Thy Heaven of Praise. O Lord! Verily she is poor and seeking the Ocean of Thy Grace; sorrowful and desiring the shelter of Thy Mercy; humble and imploring Thee at the wellspring of Thy Mercy; timid and fearful on account of her shortcomings, seeking the shelter of Thy forgiveness and pardon. O Lord! Make her a sign of forgiveness in the Kingdom and swift to attain Thy Pardon and Beneficence at Thy sacred Threshold. Verily Thou art the Generous, the Merciful, the Compassionate.

Her husband, Hájí Mírzá Ibrahím, who was known in the family as Hájí Mírzá Buzurg (the older Hájí Mírzá, to distinguish him from the second husband of Khadíjih) lived on until 1938.

Their son Amínu'lláh was very naughty as a child. Zoghollah remembers on one occasion in the Tarbiyat school, Amínu'llah had done something wrong and Dr Mesbah called out to one of the *farrashes* of the school: "Áqá Shukru'lláh! Bring the bastinado." As Amínu'llah was lying there being beaten, he suddenly reached up, seized Áqá Shukru'lláh by the testes and squeezed hard. Áqá Shukru'lláh let go of the bastinado and Amínu'lláh ran away and never came to the school again.[89]

He later trained in medicine and became known to everyone as Dr. Ulfat. Nirvana Fleming writes: "He used to mix old remedies and new science. For instance

---

89 Zoghollah Momen, interview, 21 April 2001.

if we had a cold and simple childhood problems, he would write a prescription of different herbs for different ailment and give it to Mom. Two doors down from his office there was a store like a pharmacy that carried all that, and he would put the herbs together per the prescription."[90]

Years later, his Bahá'í administrative rights were removed because he had a Muslim marriage. Later he tried to enter politics and become a member of parliament, banking on the influence of the father of his third wife, Shaykh 'Abdu'l-Husayn Najmabadi, but he did not succeed in this.

Dr Ulfat had just one daughter from his first marriage with Batul Khanum. Her name was Viyulit (Violette) or Simin. She was never a Bahá'í. She was however, very keen to marry Sedratollah but neither he nor Eshghollah would agree to this. She married twice, had five children and lives in Eastbourne, where they own three shops next to each other, just outside the station, a one-hour photographic developer, a Belgian chocolate shop and another shop.

---

90 Nirvana Behrouzmand, email 15 August 2016.

'Alí Ulfat

'Alí Ulfat was the third child of Áqá Muhammad Husayn and Fátimih-Sughrá. He was born in Yazd in about 1882. It is likely that he was born just after his parents had become Bahá'ís since he was given the name 'Alí Muhammad and he is addressed by that name in the tablets of 'Abdu'l-Bahá. He was always called just 'Alí, however, by the family. When he grew up, he assisted his father at his pharmacy and perfumery shop in the Yazd bazaar.

When the Yazd upheaval of 1903 occurred, 'Alí was a young man of about 21 years. He was not married at this time. On the first day of the Yazd upheaval, 13 June 1903, the mob came to the shop in search of his father. It happened that Áqá Muhammad Husayn was out of the shop but 'Alí was there. Fortunately the mob did not harm him and left. As he saw the deteriorating situation, 'Alí shut up shop and hurried home to warn his father. The two of them left home just as the mob arrived. They hurried away up one street as the mob descended upon the house down the next.

Áqá Muhammad Husayn went off and took refuge at the house of the Afnáns. Word reached 'Alí that the mob was looking for "'Alí-yi Bábí" to kill him. Not knowing what to do, he took off into the underground water channels that ran beneath the houses in Yazd. In most of the houses in that part of town, there would be a flight of some 50 steps down to these underground water channels that brought the water to Yazd from a system of qanáts. Because it was always cold at this level, people would also store food here.

'Alí put his young brother Muhammad Labib on his shoulders and descended into these underground water channels in search of safety. Khadíjih Ulfat states that:

> They were in the water channels for two months. Labib was on his shoulders. But he had to give Labib back because he could not take him into the waters in the dark night. So he came and gave Labib to the family of 'Alí Chahársú'í who were Bahá'ís.[91]
>
> He went to one house and they said to him: "Go away! They have said that anyone who keeps a Bábí in their house, we will fall upon his house and destroy it and take away whatever he has. And we will kill anyone who keeps a Bábí in his house." And so these people were afraid. One woman had suckled my older brother when he was a baby and my mother's milk was not sufficient. They were neighbours and she would come once or twice a day to give him milk. And so when 'Alí came to a place in the underground water-channels that he knew to be their house, he came up at night. She would light a fire to dry out his clothes. When his clothes were dry, she would give him a meal which he ate. She would then give him some tea, which he would drink, then they would send him off again into the underground water-channels. He continued in

---

91 Khadíjih Ulfat interview, transcript by Mahin Vahdat, p. 18. Khadíjih Khanum goes on to say: "Mashhadi Hasan, his wife and daughter came here and were guests of my mother. They said that ['Alí Chahársú'í] had been cut into quarters and hung from trees and gates and houses so that the people could see it."

this way for some time.[92]

Khadíjih Ulfat recall that one day, while they were staying at the house of her brother-in-law and sister, Sakínih, in the Vaqt-u-Sá'at quarter, a dirty and dishevelled figure, whom she did not recognize came up to her:

> One day when we were in the house of my relatives in the Vaqt-u-Sá'at quarter, we saw a man coming with a spade over his shoulder, a scarf around his head, a old pair of shoes (*gívih*) on his feet, and a cloth wrapped around his legs, wet up to here. He had a beard growing. He entered our house. I asked him: "Who are you?". He laughed and said "It is I. Don't you recognised me?" I said: "No." He said: "I have come out of the ditch. If I had come differently. You would have seen me and known me. I have become this colour so as to seem like a water-worker." He came and stood. I gave him some tea. I gave him some bread. He had these and then went again. He could not stay . . . Gradually, bit by bit, he came out [of his underground hiding-place].[93]

When the family came to Tehran in about 1905, 'Ali also came with them, but shortly after that, he left for Kirman where he lived for many years. He worked as a teacher there and married Khánum Sultán Kirmání, who was not a Bahá'í. They had one daughter, Mihrangíz, called Mihrí. They owned a large house and garden.

Their daughter Mihrí married Sohrab Labib, the son of Muhammad Labib in Tehran in 1945. 'Alí and his wife moved to Tehran in 1956 after he retired, living in

---

92 Khadíjih Ulfat interview, transcript by Mahin Vahdat, pp. 9-10
93 Khadíjih Ulfat interview, transcript by Mahin Vahdat, p. 10.

the house of Áqá Muhammad Husayn Ulfat. The house had been inherited by his children. Mahin had purchased her mother and Khadíjih's portions of the house and gave this to Mihri. Mihri pulled down that old house in about 1962 and built a new house on the site. 'Ali Ulfat died in Tehran on 16 May 1957 and was buried in Gulistán-i Jávíd. His wife died the following year and was buried in Imámzádih 'Abdu'lláh.

Vadí'ih Momen

Vadí'ih Momen was the fourth surviving child of Áqá Muhammad Husayn and Fátimih-Sughrá. She was born in Yazd in 1891, just at the time when the episode of the Seven Martyrs of Yazd occurred. She was given the name Ruqiyyih at birth and this is the name mentioned by 'Abdu'l-Bahá in tablets to the family; her husband gave her the name Vadí'ih at the time of their marriage; to her children and grandchildren she was known as "Mámí". She was 12 years old when the upheaval of 1903 took place. She was present and witnessed the destruction of the family home and the days of terror and uncertainty that followed. One day during that upheaval, the governor of Yazd, Jalálu'd-Dawlih, sent some of his men with a plate of pilaw rice to the wrecked house of Áqá Muhammad Husayn Ulfat, to try to re-assert his authority on the situation. One of those who came to the house on that occasion was a young man, aged about 23, who was a *píshkár* (steward) for Jalálu'd-Dawlih. His name was Muhammad Momen and he was from Shiraz. This was how Muhammad got to know the family. He also worked as *pishkár* for the Dihqán family.[94]

Two or three years later (1905 or 1906), Vadí'ih accompanied her mother and siblings to Tehran. It was a long way and took 33 days. They rode in *kajávihs* (litters) on mules and asses. Muhammad Labib recalls

---

94 Notes by Moojan Momen of a conversation with Muhammad Labib at London Airport, 15 October 1979.

that he and Vadí'ih were the youngest two children and a mischievous pair. One day, during the journey, they had wondered why it was that candles were always lit by night and not by day. So they made a tent out of blankets and lit candles inside this. Of course the whole thing went up in flames and their mother had to throw both of them into a pond to put out their burning clothes.[95]

Some years after their arrival in Tehran, Muhammad Momen asked for the hand of Vadí'ih. They were married in 1913. Muhammad Momen was born in 1880 (1259 AHSh) in Shiraz, the son of Hájí Áqá Khán and Shírín Khánum. He became a Bahá'í but all of his family in Shiraz were Muslims and so Muhammad and Vadí'ih's children never got to know that side of the family. It was Muhammad Momen who gave his wife the name Vadí'ih. The surname Momen came from Muhammad's grandfather in Shiraz who had been known as Mullá Muhammad Mu'min.

It appears that in about 1921, Muhammad Momen contemplated taking up a career in journalism. The following message was, however, conveyed to him from 'Abdu'l-Bahá, through his mother-in-law:

> Haifa, 5/10/21
> Through Hajji Amín,
> To the Maid-servant of God, the wife of Áqá Muhammad Husayn 'Attár Yazdí
>
> . . .
>
> Give most glorious (*abhá*) and most wondrous greetings from me to His Honour Áqá Muhammad Momen and send him my warmest love. I pray to God that means

---

95 Notes by Moojan Momen of a conversation with Muhammad Labib at London Airport, 15 October 1979.

will become available so that he may succeed in being of service. However he should not waste his time with writing articles for local newspapers, for this is fruitless and has no beneficial result. It brings no joy or gladness. I have written briefly, please excuse me.
Upon thee be the glory of glories.[96]

Muhammad Momen joined the Department of the Treasury. Their first child Mahboubeh was born in Tehran in 1914. Soon, Muhammad Momen was sent to be the Financial Controller of the Department's offices in Sabzivár (where Sedratollah was born in 1916), Shahrúd (where Eshghollah was born in 1918), Simnan, Burújird (in 1922 where Majzoub was born in 1924). Zoghollah remembers that when they were setting off for Burujird, Ahmad Aqa had Zoghollah in his arms and was saying: "Don't forget this one." They travelled by cart (*gári*).

Muhammad Momen died in Burújird in early 1927 as a result of blood loss from haemorrhoids. Vadí'ih returned to Tehran at this time, by cart and pregnant. Zoghollah remembers that there were a lot of lights up in Tehran as they entered the town and Esghollah told him this was because of Reza Shah's coronation.[97] Mahin was born in July 1927 in Tehran a few months after her father's passing.

The rest of Vadí'ih's life was concerned with the raising of her children. It was a difficult task for a young woman to raise 6 young children in Iran. She received a great deal of support from her father, mother and sister, Khadíjih. She lived in their house when she first returned to Tehran and they continued to assist her

---
96 From typed copy of tablet in possession of Mahin Vahdat.
97 Zoghollah Momen, interview, 14 March 2004.

until their deaths. Vadí'ih in turn supported her daughter Mahboubeh when she had problems during her first pregnancy in 1934. Vadí'ih used to go to English classes given by Dr Moody or Keith Ransom-Kehler.

Towards the end of her life, Vadí'ih had a series of strokes. The first of these was in summer 1955, shortly after Mahboubeh and Gloria had left for England. She was sitting down in the house of Khálih Khanum and started to scratch at ears and then fell unconscious. She was taken to the Mehr Hospital. After this she was nursed for a time by Rúhá, who had previously been Moojan and Hooman's nurse. She had a series of strokes.

In about 1957, Vadí'ih moved in with her youngest daughter Mahin Vahdat and her husband. She had a stroke in about 1962 which left her with difficulty in finding the right words to say (dysphasia). Despite this, she attended the Bahá'í World Congress in London in 1963. Zoghollah wanted her at that time to stay with him in Rimini but Mahin said that it would be too difficult for Bahiyyih to cope and she returned to Tehran. In about 1964, when Mahin wanted to go on a trip to visit Nika in Spain, Vadí'ih went to live with her second daughter, Majzoub. She died in Majzoub's house in Tehran in November 1966.

Muhammad Labib

Muhammad Labib was the fifth and youngest surviving child of Áqá Muhammad Husayn and Fátimih-Sughrá. He was born in Yazd in 1894. He was named Muhammad Mahdi at birth and this is the name by which he is addressed in tablets of 'Abdu'l-Bahá. When surnames became compulsory, he took the surname Labib, as 'Abdu'l-Bahá had said to him: *"tu labíbí, tu labíbí"* (You are wise, you are wise). Mehri Molin writes:

> When the birth certificate became mandatory, father was in Qazvin away from the rest of the family. He chose several names and one night he had a dream that he placed all the names in between the pages of the book of Aqdas and drew one, which was Labib and prior to his dream he actually opened the Book of Aqdas and, at the beginning of one of the pages, Labib (which means wise) appeared, so he added Labib to the rest of the names. For final approval he wrote to Abdul-Baha about it.[98]

During the 1903 upheaval, his older brother lifted him up onto to his shoulders and went down into the underground water channels.

> I was nine years old in those days, when with my brother and several other of the friends, we spent several days in an underground water ditch fleeing from those

---

98 Mehri Molin, email 29 April 2001.

evil people. Then we took refuge in the deep, damp, underground cellars of some non-Bahá'í friends.[99]

Muhammd Labib came with the rest of the family to Tehran in 1905. He was enrolled first in the American Protestant school and then in the newly opened Bahá'í school, the Tarbiyat school. When he was 14 (i.e. 1908), he also started attending the Bahá'í education classes taught by the eminent Bahá'í poet and teacher Na'ím. Later he also attended Bahá'í classes held by Shaykh Kázim Samandar, Mírzá 'Azízu'lláh Misbáh, and Fádil Mázandarání. Eventually 12 of the students of these classes, including Muhammad Labíb, established a class for teaching the Bahá'í Faith to the students at the Tarbiyat School. Sidney Sprague, who taught English at the Tarbiyat School, wanted to encourage these students and so he sent a petition to 'Abdu'l-Bahá, asking for his blessings on this group of 12. 'Abdu'l-Bahá replied with a tablet saying that he was praying for them, that they should be thankful to be in such a school and encouraging them to dedicate themselves to the service of the Faith.

'Abdu'l-Bahá was encouraging the Bahá'ís to gain a knowledge of English and Muhammad Labíb diligently studied this language with Sidney Sprague and became familiar with it. In 1914, he also began to study Esperanto with Bahman Shaydání, who had learned the language while abroad. The arrival of tablets from 'Abdu'l-Bahá encouraging the learning of Esperanto redoubled his enthusiasm for this task. After two months, Muhammad Labíb was himself teaching a class of Bahá'í and non-Bahá'í youth Esperanto classes.

---

99 Muhammad Labib, *Khátirát-i Shast Rúzih*, manuscript, p. 6.

In 1916, Muhammad Labíb was asked to go to Qazvin to teach in the Tavakkul School, the Bahá'í school there. As well as teaching English in the Tavakkul School, Muhammad Labíb set up Esperanto classes in Qazvin and established contact with the international head-quarters of the Esperanto movement in Switzerland. In the International Esperanto Year-Book of that period, he is listed as the official representative for Qazvin.

Muhammad Labíb also taught Bahá'í education classes for the children. It was as a result of this activity that it occurred to him to set up a savings fund for the children, the Shirkat-i Nawnahálán (The Children's Company). This was discussed in the Bahá'í community and the suggestion sent off to 'Abdu'l-Bahá, who approved it. He began its work informally in 1917.

Then in 1919, Muhammad Labíb accompanied his father to the presence of 'Abdu'l-Bahá in Haifa. Although pilgrimages were usually only for 9 days, 'Abdu'l-Bahá gave permission for them to remain for 60 days. Muhammad Labíb has written a detailed account of the 60 days that he spent there. Among the matters that were raised by 'Abdu'l-Bahá was the Shirkat-i Nawnhálán. Not only did 'Abdu'l-Bahá give his approval, but he revealed a prayer for the fund, gave instructions that it be established formally and officially, gave instructions on it workings, and he gave a contribution of two gold coins to the fund. Four of Muhammad Labíb's fellow-pilgrims, one from each of four continents, each gave a contribution of two pounds, John Esslemont from England (Europe), George Latimer from the United States (America), Shaykh Faraju'lláh Kurdí from Egypt (Africa), and Mirzá Muhammad Hasan of the pilgrim house (Asia). One year later the official head-quarters of this fund were established in Tehran, and it remained an important part of the Iranian Bahá'í community until the Revolution of 1979. Muhammad Labib continued to receive guidance from 'Abdu'l-Bahá regarding the education of children and the Nawnhálán Company and he received some five Tablets in all.

In September 1921, Labib married Shawqiyyih, the daughter of Aqa Husayn 'Alí Mi'már-báshí, a Bahá'í of Qazvin. 'Abdu'l-Bahá sent a message saying:

> The marriage of Mírzá Muhammad Labíb and the daughter of Áqá Husayn 'Alí Mi'már-Báshí is blessed. I beseech God that, through the Grace of Bahá'u'lláh, they may establish a blessed family.[100]

They had 10 children and also adopted one child (Ehsan). Their oldest daughter Rawshan was a great help to her mother in raising the children. They were in Hamadan in 1923, in Kermanshah 1926-31, in Tehran in the 1930s, and in Abadan in 1944. During all this time, Labib was in receipt of at least sixteen letters written on behalf of Shoghi Effendi and one from Bahiyyih Khanum.

Muhammad Labíb was a keen photographer and took photographs of many Bahá'í holy places. In 1930-31, he accompanied Effie Baker around Iran, when she was taking the photographs that would eventually illustrate *Nabil's Narrative*. He worked for the Iranian oil company at first in Tehran and was stationed in Abadan in the 1940s.

Labib was on pilgrimage to visit Shoghi Effendi

---

100 Tablet to Dr Susan Moody, dated 2 October 1921. It was sent by Shoghi Effendi after the passing of 'Abdu'l-Bahá.

in 1953 and has left an account of that pilgrimage. He pioneered to Hiroshima in 1955. He remained in the Far East for nine years. Then in 1963, he pioneered to Rhodes in the Mediterranean. In about 1968, he returned to Tehran and wrote his memoires and several other books. One of these, *The Seven Martyrs of Hurmuzak*, has been translated into English and published.

He visited the United States in the 1970s. Nahid Azad (the daughter-in-law of Mr Labib's eldest daughter Roshan) writes:

> When I first met him in summer of 1975 at his daughter's house Roushan, I was so touched by his positive attitude about life and his mission for the Bahá'í Faith. Although he was loosing his eyesight he never complained. As a matter of fact I remember that he used to say: "It was good that I lost my eyesight. If this didn't happen I would still be travel teaching and would never sit somewhere to finish my books." On March 26, 1979 after the revolution of Iran, I , with my two daughters left Tehran in a 747 to London and New York. In that trip Mr. Muhammad Labib was with us. At that time the Iranian government was not giving permission to men to leave Iran. In that 747 plane leaving Teheran there were women and children. I remember Mr. Labib was the only man traveling. He went to New York to get medical help for his eyesight. He was such a pleasurable person to be with and travel with. He was positive, loving and did not ever complain. That trip was the last time I saw him.[101]

After completing his medical treatment, Mr Labib returned to Iran, via London, in October 1979. During his

---

101 Nahid Azad e-mail 20 March 2001.

brief stopover at Lonon Airport, he met with Mahboubeh Khanum, Moojan Momen, Wendi Momen and their two children. He died in Tehran on 14 March 1981.

The Universal House of Justice sent the following cable on his passing:

> SADDENED NEWS PASSING DEVOTED SERVANT SACRED THRESHOLD MUHAMMAD LABIB. HIS DEDICATED LONGSTANDING RECORD SERVICES IRAN REMEMBERED WITH DEEP APPRECIATION. ASSURE RELATIVES FERVENTLY PRAYING SHRINES PROGRESS HIS SOUL ABHA KINGDOM.[102]

---

102 *Bahá'í World,* vol. 18, 1979-1981, (Haifa: Bahá'í World Center, 1986), pp. 751-2.

Mahboubeh Kouchekzadeh

Mahboubeh Khanum was born in Tehran probably in 1914 (although her passport and gravestone say 1911), the eldest child of Vadí'ih and Muhammad Momen. Because, during her childhood, her father was posted to different parts of the country, Mahboubeh (Mahboubeh Khanum or Mahboub Ján as she was known in the family) stayed with her grandfather, Áqá Muhammad Husayn Ulfat in Tehran so that she could go to school. She attended the Tarbiyat School for Girls.

Mahboubeh was in her final year at the Tarbiyat School in 1933, when the American Bahá'í, Keith Ransom Kehler came to Iran. She asked to speak to the final year students at the school. She came into their classroom and gave a talk during which she encouraged them to remove the *chádor* (the cloak worn by women in public and pulled across the face). Someone in the audience spoke up and said that Shoghi Effendi had advised that the Bahá'ís should not be at the forefront of such moves since it would inevitably cause public agitation. Keith replied that although he had said that Bahá'ís should not be at the forefront, he had not said that the Bahá'ís should at the tail-end either. Already at that time, it was the custom among some of the wealthier women to walk about the richer northern areas of Tehran without a *chádor*. What Keith was suggesting, however, that the Bahá'í girls, most of whom at that time lived in central or southern Tehran, go without a *chádor* was daring and possibly dangerous.

Mahboubeh returned home, enthused by this talk, and said to her grand-father that she wanted to go without the *chádor*. Her grand-father had no objections. He cited the tablet that his wife had received from 'Abdu'l-Bahá after she had been dragged into the street and been publically shamed and humiliated by having her chádor removed. 'Abdu'l-Baha had written a tablet in which he comforted her and said that her "bare-headedness is the highest degree of chastity and purity (*'iffat*)." Áqá Muhammad Husayn regarded this tablet as evidence that the family had permission from 'Abdu'l-Bahá to go without the *chádor*. So from that day, Mahboubeh discarded the *chádor* – although she said that she continued to wear a *chádor* as she left the house until she got to the end of Malek Road because there was a stern old mullá living at the end of the road.[103]

When Mahboubeh Khanum finished school, she was asked to stay on as a teacher. The following year, she was married to Jamshid Kouchekzadeh, a Bahá'í from a Zoroastrian family of Kirman. He had himself become a Bahá'í in Bombay and had returned to Iran to tell his family. His younger brother Houshang became a Bahá'í but another brother and a sister and his parents remained Zoroastrians and lived in Kerman, although they were all very friendly towards the Bahá'í Faith and the sister even used to wear a Bahá'í ring that he had given her.[104] Mr Kouchekzadeh then decided to cycle from Kerman to Tehran to seek work. In those days the British were

---

103 Related by Mahboubeh Kouchekzadeh in Summer 1996 in Leidschendam.
104 Related by Mahin Vahdat 24 January 2004.

fixing a telegragh wire across Iran to India and they had camps all along the route. He knew a little English and would stop at each camp, talk to the head of the camp and stay the night until he arrived in Tehran.[105] In his early days he had joined the South Iran Force set up by the British. Later he was in charge of accounts at the printing press of the Iranian Parliament (*Chápkhánih-yi Majlis*). Mahboubeh's uncle Muhammad Labib knew Mr Kouchekzadeh and knew that he had wanted to get married and so he introduced him to Mahboubeh Khanum.[106] Mr Kouchekzadeh remained in this job until his retirement and was very highly regarded by his colleagues and superiors.

Again at Keith Ransom Kehler's suggestion, the marriage ceremony and reception was held with all of the male and female guests freely intermingling and with the women not wearing the chádor. This was, to the best of my aunt's knowledge, the first occasion in which this had happened in a large Bahá'í gathering. Also it was the first time that there was dancing in the Western style at a wedding. It may, in addition, have been one of the earliest marriages between a Bahá'í from a Zoroastrian background and a Bahá'í from a Muslim background. There is a photograph of the guests at the wedding.[107]

At first after their marriage, they lived at a house that Mr Kouchekzadeh owned on Koucheh-yi Sháhrukh, Khiyábán Nádirí. Kianush was born in that house. Later they built and moved to a house on Koucheh-yi Malik,

---

105 Shidan Kouchekzadeh, email dated 7 May 2013.
106 Related by Mahin Vahdat 24 January 2004.
107 Related by Mahboubeh Kouchekzadeh in Summer 1996 in Leidschendam.

the land for which they bought from Zinat Sadat and built on. There, they were close to Mahboubeh's mother, who was able to help her with her children. Many stories are told in the family about Mr Kouchekzadeh's fastidiousness and his exact and complete obedience of the instructions of Shoghi Effendi. For example, Shoghi Effendi had written that the Bahá'ís should support the Bahá'í schools. Mr Kouchekzadeh had two houses on Koucheh-yi Sháhrukh. He sold both of them, one of which paid for the house on Koucheh-yi Malik and the proceeds of the other house, he wanted to present to the National Spiritual Assembly for the Bahá'í schools. The only problem was that the Bahá'í schools had been closed by the government by then. So the Assembly was reluctant to take such a large donation for something that no longer existed, but Mr Kouchekzadeh was adamant that, since Shoghi Effendi had wanted the Bahá'ís to give money for the schools, they should take the money for that purpose.[108]

After her marriage, Mahboubeh Khanum was very much occupied with having and raising her children. Her first pregnancy in 1934 was very difficult for her – this was Kianush.[109] The second pregnancy resulted in a girl called Jaleh, who only lived for five or six months. Then their other two children Ida and Shidan were born. Despite these preoccupations, she was also able to pursue an active Bahá'í life. She continued her interest in the advancement of women by serving on Bahá'í women's committee (*Lajnih-yi Taraqqí-yi Nisván*), and

---

108 Story told by Zoghullah Momen in Summer 2002.
109 Information from Mahin Vahdat in interview at the home of Nika Vahdat, Madrid, April 2001.

she was also on the committee for the registration of new Bahá'ís.[110] In addition, she was a teacher of *Dars-i Akhláq* (children's Bahá'í classes) and served on the Bahá'í education committee (Lajnih Tarbiyat Amrí). Mr Kouchekzadeh was on the committee of the Bahá'í fund (*Sanduq-i Khayriyyih*), which was often convened at their house and the Statistics Committeee (*Lajnih-yi Ihsá'iyyih*). Shoghi Effendi had recommended England as the best place for schooling and so they decided to send Kianoush to England (January 1950).

Mahboubeh Khanum was always very chic. Because she was short, she had to have her clothes and shoes made for her. So she used to have them made copying the styles from catalogues from abroad. As a result, she always wore the latest fashions. She sometimes wore clothes that seemed strange at the time but later they became the style that everyone wore. For example, one Naw-Ruz, she wore a dress that was half-yellow and half-brown, with a hat and bag to match. It was very striking. Later it became the fashion. She was very good at making clothes and also at knitting. She would make her own clothes from patterns from Europe.[111] She was very talented in this way and if she saw a picture of a dress she liked, she was often able to make it up herself. She also made her own hats and once even made a coat for herself. She would also sometimes get a dress-maker such as Qudsiyyih Mazlum to make clothes for her.[112]

In about 1952, Mr Kouchekzadeh took early retirement from government work. At this time,

---

110 Shidan Kouchekzadeh, e-mail of 10 June 2001.
111 Taped interview with Victoria Afshar, 3 February 2001.
112 Related by Mahin Vahdat, 24 January 2004.

Shoghi Effendi called for the convening of a number of intercontinental conferences and asked everyone to make an effort to go to them. The first of these conferences was in February 1953 in Kampala. Mr Kouchekzadeh could not afford the airfare from Tehran to Kampala, but was determined to obey Shoghi Effendi, so he decided, despite his age, to go overland to Kampala. This took him two months, going by road to Baghdad then across Syria; catching a boat to Egypt, down the Nile by boat; and finally by road to Kampala. He arrived the night before the conference began. Everyone was surprised to see him as no-one had thought he would make it, and Mr Furutan congratulated him.[113]

In October 1953 the last of the intercontinental conferences called by Shoghi Effendi to mark the Holy Year took place. On this occasion it was Mahboubeh Khanum who did an epic journey overland from Tehran to Delhi. She took a group of eight to ten Bahá'ís (amongst them Mr Khadem's mother in law and Mr Behjat – later a pioneer to Africa: Ivory coast and Mauretania). She went on a local regular transport bus from Tehran to Mashad. In Mashad a friend of Sedratollah (who was the commander in that town) helped them to find a bus driver and ensured their safety from Mashad to Zahedan. In those days it was very unsafe as it is today on the border of Iran and Afghanstan. From Zahedan they took a train to Karachi and then to Delhi. You can see Mahboubeh Khanum sitting next to Mrs Khadem in the picture of the conference hanging in one the rooms of the Bahji mansion.[114]

---

113 Shidan Kouchekzadeh, email dated 7 May 2013.
114 Shidan Kouchekzadeh, email dated 7 May 2013.

After Mr Kouchekzadeh's retirement, he had wanted to go pioneering to Afghanistan but this did not prove possible. Eventually Mahboubeh Khanum came overland to England in August 1955, in order to be with her two older children who were already studying in that country. She travelled with her younger son, Shidan, Gloria Momen, and her two sons Moojan and Hooman. They settled in Bournemouth. Mr Kouchekzadeh remained behind to wind up their affairs and to sell their house, but he fell ill with his diabetes. Majzoub wrote to Mahboubeh saying that Mr Kouchekzadeh was seriously ill. She replied to send him to England where he could get better treatment and so he left to join Mahboubeh Khanum in England. He spent several months in Boscombe Hospital, Bournemouth. After this Mahboubeh Khanum returned for a short trip and sold their house.

Another story about Mr Kouchekzadeh relates to the time that he was moving from Iran to England. He was very ill at this time from diabetes and leg ulcers that would not heal despite prolonged treatment. Zoghollah Momen was one of those who took him to Tehran Airport and put him onto the aeroplane to go to England. He had on his arms a suit and some other clothes and Zoghollah took hold of them to hand them to the airline staff to look after, but Mr Kouchekzadeh refused to let them go. It was explained to him that they would be quite safe and would be handed back to him at the end of the flight, but he still adamantly refused to be parted from them and was getting very worked up about this. As he was quite ill and weak, Zoghollah did not know what to do, so he asked him why he would not let go of the clothes. Mr Kouchezadeh explained that the flight would be flying over the Holy Land and Haifa and Shoghi Effendi had said that when the Bahá'ís came to the Holy Land, they should put on new clothes, so he wanted to do this as the plane flew over the Holy Land.[115]

In 1956, they moved to Canford Cliffs and lived with Eileen Beales, a Bahá'í who had a house overlooking the sea and the cliffs there. When Eileen Beales decided to move away for purposes of pioneering, they moved to a flat in Westbourne. Kianoush Kouchekzadeh writes:

> It was at this address that the final decision came from the Home Office, refusing them the extension of their visas.
>
> My father and mother then moved to Dublin some time in late summer of 1957. They were living in Dublin and I, in Bradford, when in November 1957 the news of the passing of the Beloved Guardian reached us. I went and picked them up with my little car from Liverpool, to go to London for the funeral. During their stay in Dublin, they lived in a basement flat in the Ranelagh part of the city. They left Dublin in the second half of 1960 and lived for a while in Dolphin Square in London.[116]

Shidan Kouchekzadeh remembers that it was "In late October 1957 about 10 days before the passing of the Guardian" that "Maman and Baba left from the flat on Poole Road (which has been subsequently demolished) for Dublin and stayed in 14 Charleston Road [Ranelagh, Dublin]."[117] Their move to Dublin made possible the

---

115 Story told by Zoghullah Momen in Summer 2002.
116 Kianoush Kouchekzadeh, e-mail 28 May 2001.
117 Shidan Kouchekzadeh, email 10 June 2001.

formation of the first Local Spiritual Assembly of Dublin.

In October 1960, the whole family drove by car to Istanbul and then on to make the pilgrimage to the Holy Land. From there, Mahboubeh went on to Iran, where she remained for about a year. From here she arranged her son Kianoush's marriage in February 1961 and then flew to Vienna to attend her daughter Ida's marriage in November 1961.

Shidan Kouchekzadeh writes: "In June 1963 after my wedding in Bounemouth, Maman went to Ida in Vienna and then came back to collect the belongings with Baba and settled in Vienna." Ida Farid writes:

> In the summer of 1963 Maman came to Vienna to be with me as Gian was just one month old. After a couple of months she left again to go back . . . in order to make arrangements for her return (with my father) to Austria to help us to look after Gian while I worked. My parents stayed in Vienna for approximately 2 years. Gian was then sent to a nursery school and they were free to choose to stay in Austria or go back to England. At this time uncle Eshghu'llah and Gitti came from Persia to stay with us. After a few months my parents decided to pioneer to a nearby town called Klosterneuburg. They stayed in Klosterneuburg for approximately 2 years after which they (and Gitti) went back to England to live in Cheadle, Cheshire, and uncle Ishghu'llah went back to Persia.[118]

When their son Shidan went off pioneering with his wife Susan to Sierra Leone in September 1966, their house in Cheadle, near Manchester, was put on the market but

---

118 Ida Farid, e-mail of 9 June 2001.

failed to sell. In early 1967, Mahboubih and her husband decided to move into that house. Guitty Momen joined them and went to school. In September 1969, they moved to a flat in Watford near their son, Kianoush. Kianoush Kouchekzadeh writes about the last years of Mahboubih and Jamshid Kouchekzadeh thus:

> . . . they moved to Watford to occupy their own flat at 39 the Spinney, Church Road. On 31st December 1971, my father passed away at the age of 72, after becoming ill with infuenza followed by complications. Maman stayed on in Watford and she had to suffer the trauma of my divorce with Parvin. Early in 1973, I moved to the Netherlands. Maman came to live with me, in Oegstgeest, from January 1974 until February 1975, when I married Jinus Azami.[119] She came on regular visits to Holland, especially when my children with Parvin, Ramin and Mona, came to stay with me. In April of 1976, she suffered the shock of losing her grandchildren in the road accident. She attended the Paris conference in August of that year and came to stay with us for a while, when Jinus gave birth to Ramin in October 1976. She returned to Watford.[120]

Mahboubeh continued to live in Watford until 1985. At this time she had an episode of vomiting up blood due to some Ibuprofen tablets that she had been taking. She also suffered from high blood pressure. Kianoush

---

[119] Jinus Azami's maternal grandfather was Muhmmad Husayn Rawhani (father of Enayat) who was charged by Shoghi Effendi with finding and relocating the remains of Baha'u'llah's father in Karbila, which he did. Jinus' paternal grandmother Tuba Azami, lost her uncle and grandfather at Shaykh Tabarsi upheaval as martyrs.
[120] Kianoush Kouchekzadeh, e-mail 28 May 2001.

Kouchekzadeh writes:

> In 1985 it became clear that she should not live alone without help being close at hand. Her preference was to come to the Netherlands and stay close to us. She lived in a flat owned by Shidan, then moved to a flat for the elderly and finally to a nursing home in 1997, where she passed away in [15] February 1998.[121]

---

121 Kianoush Kouchekzadeh, e-mail 28 May 2001.

Sedratollah Momen

Sedratollah (Sidratu'lláh) was the second oldest child of Vadí'ih and Muhammad Momen. He was born in 1916 in Sabzivar, where his father was posted at the time. Muhammad Labib recounted that Vadí'ih wanted to call him Sirru'llah but 'Abdu'l-Bahá appeared to her in a dream and said to call him Sedratollah.[122]

He attended the Bahá'í Tarbiyat School in Tehran. Zoghollah Momen remembers one story about that school. The *názim* (person responsible for order in the school) was Mirza Murtada Khan Danesh (Dr Danesh). He used to sit overlooking the play area, but he had dark glasses and so no-one could tell whether he was asleep or awake. So much of the time he would snooze away. One time a fight broke out between two of the boys in the playground and the other boys gathered around egging them on. Then Sedratollah jumped forward to separate the two boys. Just at this time Danesh woke up and thought that it was Sedratollah who was fighting and ran up and hit him across the back of the head. Sedratollah was incensed at the injustice of this and struck Danesh back. This was scandalous and unheard of in the school for a pupil to hit the *názim*. Everyone gasped. Sedratollah was taken before Mesbah (the headmaster) and summarily expelled from the school without any further questions being asked. Sedratollah went home and explained what

---

122 Interview, Muhammad Labib at Heathrow Airport, London, 7 October 1979.

had happened to his grand-father, Aqa Muhammad Husayn Ulfat. The latter had some considerable status in the Bahá'í community. So he went to the school and saw Dr Mesbah to explain what had happened. Eventually Sedratollah was allowed back into the school.[123] After the Tarbiyat school was closed by the Government in 1934 when he was 19 years old, he began to attend the Military School – Madrasih-yi Nizám (which was for classes 7-12).

Sedratollah then entered the Dánishkadih Afsarí (Military Academy), from which he graduated after two years. He entered the Iranian Air Force and trained to be a pilot. He went up through the ranks – Setván (lieutenant) 3, Setván 2, Setván 1, then Sarván (captain), and was Sarhang 2 (lieutenant-colonel) when he passed away. He trained as a pilot in Tehran and loved to fly. His mother asked him why he had chosen such a dangerous career and he replied: "Mother, our life is not in our own hands it is in God's hand. At whatever time he wishes He will end our life, whether I be in the air or on the ground." But his mother was always very worried about his flying. Although many Bahá'ís were expelled from the armed forces in about about 1940, it appears that his senior officers protected him from this. He was stationed at first in Kurdistan and Kermanshah and later, after his marriage, in Tabriz.

Sedratollah was very involved in Bahá'í community activities. He was on the youth committee and was the convenor of a 19-Day Feast in the Hasanabad area.[124] Shafiqih FatheAzam related to Zoghollah that one time

---

123 Interview Zoghollah Momen, London, 21 April 2001.
124 Related by Mahin Vahdat 24 January 2004.

she was at a youth gathering and a young man came in wearing military uniform and looking very smart. When everyone got up to introduce themselves he said he was Sedratollah Momen. Shafiqih got very excited at this because her sister had recently married Eshghollah and at the break went up to him and said: "Are you Sedratollah Momen?" And he had said: "Yes." So she said: "I am Shafiqih, Jazbi's sister. And he had said: "Jazbi?" – seeming to be unaware of who Jazbi was. Shafiqih said: "I felt so embarrassed having gone up to him so enthusiastically that I wished the ground could swallow me up."

Everyone however was very concerned that Sedratollah had still not married. His two younger sisters had been married for a few years and had children and even his younger brother Eshghollah was already married. Once he related a dream that he had had that his grandfather Aqa Muhammad Husayn Ulfat had spoken to him about getting married and Mahboubeh used this as an opportunity to urge him to give this urgent attention. The family attended the same 19-Day Feast in Tehran as Gloria Iman's family and they had seen each other at these meetings, although Sedratollah was often away on account of his work. Eventually Mahboubeh and Mahin called on Gloria's parents and brought up the question of marriage. Gloria agreed and the wedding took place on 20 April 1949 in a house near the family home which had a large garden.

Sedratollah was then transferred by the military to Tabriz in November 1949 and there two children were born, Moojan and Hooman in 1950 and 1952. Sedratollah's mother came to Tabriz to be with Gloria.

Also while in Tabriz, Sedratollah attended the

Danishkadih Adabiyyat and obtained his degree in Persian Literature. He was always very good at composition and literary matters. Mahin remembers that whenever she had a composition (*inshá'*) to do for her homework, she would go to Sedratollah and ask him about it. She remembers one time she had to do a composition under the title of the feelings of a girl who is a pilot. She went to Sedratollah and said she had no idea what to write. So he said: alright write this down. And he dictated a marvellous composition a part of which Mahin has always remembered especially everytime she boards an aeroplane: "Is it possible that I too should climb aboard this beautiful bird and travel through this limitless space? (*Áyá mumkin ast man-ham bar ín parandeh-yi zíbá savár shudih, va dar ín fadá-yi lá-yatanáhí sayr namáyam?*)." When she took this composition to school, she got 18/20 for it and everyone praised it greatly.

Shortly after Hooman was born they returned to Tehran. Their house was in the hands of people who had rented it and when those people left, they spent some time decorating it and fitting up. Unfortunately, Sedratollah hardly lived in the house – the first major time that people went to the house as guests was for his memorial service.

Two days before his death, Mahin Vahdat had come to Tehran from Sari. She went first to her husband's family home. Then she came to see her own mother and heard a sound of wailing from somewhere near-by. She asked: what is going on? They told her that Sedratollah has stomachache. He had had a flight but when he went to work, he developed abdominal pain and returned home. A doctor from the military had come and had prescribed some medicine. But that had not helped. Then Dr Ulfat had been brought to him who had said that he had to go to hospital. Dr Najmabadi, Prof. Hakim and Prof. 'Adl had attended as well and they were agreed he had to go to hospital. He was taken to the Mithaqiyyih Hospital and an operation was carried out.

The afternoon of that day (1 Shahrivar, 23 August 1953) at about 2pm Mahin had gone to the hospital and Sedratollah was asleep. Mahboubeh was at his bedside. Gloria had remained at home to feed Hooman. Mahin asked: "How is he?" Mahboubeh said: "He is asleep but I want to wake him to give him some water because his mouth is very dry." She was soaking cotton wool in water and putting it to his mouth. So Mahboubeh called: "Sedratollah, Sedratollah." And he awoke a little startled and said: "Why did you wake me up? I was having a dream. I was dreaming of Hadrat-i Bahá'u'lláh, who was standing somewhere full of light. I was going to him. He said: 'Come this way.' He was guiding me how to come to Him. I was going to Him when you woke me up." Mahin had thought it was a good sign that he had had a dream of Baha'u'llah. And she had related this to Prof. Hakim joyfully. But he said nothing and walked away.[125] Afterwards Mahboubeh said she had been very upset by this dream. She had realised that he was about to die.

Gradually everyone gathered around his bedside: his mother, Gloria and their children, Mahboubeh, Majzoub, Nirvana, Mahin, Nika and others. When they were leaving he kissed everyone and said good-bye and then said to his mother: "Look after Gloria and the children." So everyone left, but Mahboubeh Khanum remained by his bedside. His mother said that she had

---

[125] Interview with Mahin, taped 7-8 April 2001.

spent the entire night walking up and down worried about what would happen. Eventually during the night news of his death reached the house. Later doctors told them that by the time they operated, his bowels had turned gangrenous and there was nothing they could do except sew him up again.[126]

It was the 2nd of Shahrivar (24 August 1952). Hooman and Farid had been born in Farvardin (March-April), some three months before and Mahin was breast-feeding Farid in her husband's family house when her cousin Sohrab Labib's son came and said: "Mahin come and let us go home." She asked: "How is Sedratollah Khan?" He replied: "Come let us go home." She had felt that something had happened but she did not think he had died. When she got to the house she learned that he had died.

Mahin remembers she cried so much that her right eye became paralysed. She went to a doctor who said it was because of her crying. One night she had a dream of Sedratullah. He said to her: "Mahin, why are you crying so much. Your tears are preventing me from entering the Kingdom. Please pray for me instead." This comforted her greatly.[127]

---

[126] There is a condition that was not well recognized then, caused by the rapid depressurization and repressurizatin that occurred when peope went up in depressurized aircraft, especially if the ascent and descent were too rapid. All military aircraft then were depressurized. The condition is caused by air bubbles forming in the arteries and veins as the pressure changes. It is called altitude decompression sickness and is similar to "diver's bends". It can cause damage to various organs and eventually death. This seems the most likely explanation of what occured to Sedratollah.

[127] Interview with Mahin, Madrid, taped 7-8 April 2001.

He had a very large funeral. The military attended with a band preceding the coffin, then the family, then his military colleagues, then other friends. They started from the hospital marched past the house in Malek Road to the turn in Khiyaban Amiriyyih and then the coffin was put in a car and taken to the Bahá'í cemetery. There was also a large memorial meeting for him hosted by Zoghollah at a place known as Maktab in Khiyaban Shah. Kamran Samimi was in charge of this place. All of his colleagues at work attended to pay their respects. There was also one in Mahboubeh's house and one in his own home. Mr Furutan had attended the memorial meeting. He had said to Mr Kouchekzadeh: "When Momen was alive, he had a love of teaching the Faith. At the time of his death, he is also teaching." This was because all of his military friends were ringing Mr Furutan up and asking for an opportunity to get some information about the Bahá'í Faith. Expressions of grief and condolences came from all parts. There was even a letter from the Bahá'ís of Kuwait, although he had never been there.

Eshghollah Momen

Eshghollah was born in 1918 in Shahrud where his father was working at the time. He attended Tarbiyat School and after this was closed went with his brother Sedratollah to the Madrasih-yi Nizám. He completed the course there, entered the army and achieved the rank of Sarhang (Colonel). Although many Bahá'ís were expelled from the armed forces in about 1940s, it appears that his senior officers protected him from this.

Eshghollah married Jazbiyyeh (Jazhbiyyih, Jazbi) Farzár in 1947. He had met her at the Haziratu'l-Quds in Tehran, where she was the secretary to Mr Furutan. Eshghollah had been a member of a committee that met there and was a member of several other committees and so came to Haziratu'l-Quds and met Jazbiyyeh. They also had friends in common, Hushyar Ashraf, Ruhollah Samandari, Houshmand FatheAzam and Mihdi Amin-Amin. Eshghollah was stationed by the Army in various parts of Iran: Gurgan, Rezaiyyeh, where Farshid was born, Kirmanshah, Abadan, where Guitty was born and where he was the assistant (*mu'ávvin*) of the military commander (*farmándár-i nizámí*), and also for a time somewhere in Mazandaran. Mr Mawzun of Kirmanshah and Mr Homayun Jalili of Ahvaz frequently spoke to Mahin Vahdat of the Bahá'í services that Eshghollah gave while in these various places. He was a member of the Local Spiritual Assemblies of Rezaiyyeh, Kirmanshah and Abadan. He was also a teacher of the Dars-Akhláq

(Bahá'í children's classes) while in Tehran.

Zoghollah remembers how on one occasion in about 1951, he was working for the railway company about 40 kilomtres from Miyaneh As it happened, at this time, Sedratollah was in charge of the Air Force stationed in Tabriz and Eshghollah was commander of the artillery in Rezaiyyeh, where there had recently been trouble with the Kurds and the Russians. Miyanih is an important railway junction with lines going towards Tehran, Tabriz and Rezaiyyeh (Urumiyyeh). Through the American President Truman's Point Four Programme, a large supply of DDT was delivered to Iran. They had sprayed the bazaar of Miyaneh with DDT, but it is highly inflammable and it had caught fire. The whole of the bazaar was alight. So they telegraphed to Sedratollah in Tabriz to fly airplanes to drop sand on the fire. Zoghollah thought of the large number of empty tin canisters in which petrol was sold and delivered. These were sitting in a warehouse waiting to be returned to be filled up again. He ordered the men working for him to take these canisters down to the river, fill them up with water and then carry them to the fire to pour on the flames. As it happened, at exactly this time, Eshghollah was taking his regiment by rail from Rezaiyyeh to Tehran. When they got to Miyanih, the train was stopped because of the fire. So Eshqullah asked what his men could do and they said to him that the best thing would be for his men to pull down buildings around the fire to stop it spreading. And so at that point in time, all three of the Momen brothers were working on the great fire of Miyanih.[128]

---

[128] Recording of interview with Zoghollah, London, 12 April 2001.

In the 1950s, many of the Iranian Baha'i families were goinging pioneering and Eshghollah and Jazbiyyeh wanted to do this also. In 1957, they decided that Jazbiyyeh and the two children move to England, where they settled in Winchester, and Eshghollah visited them from time to time. During this time, Eshghollah began a business selling electrical kitchen appliances from a shop called "Farshid". Farshid Momen writes:

> His career in the Army was cut short, due to the refusal of the Shah to grant promotion to the rank of General (Sar-tip) as recommended by his commanders. The rebuff by the Shah allied to the success of the business, Eshghollah decided to resign his commision in the Army and by 1960 he had returned to civilian life.[129]

Unfortunately, the business failed in about 1962-3 due to embezzlement and Eshghollah was bankrupted. Farshid writes:

> The failure of the business and the insidious mental disease suffered by Jazbiyyeh Khanum were the fundamental causes of the failure of their marriage which was eventually annulled in 1965.
>
> After the failure of the business and the dissolution of his marriage, Eshghollah spent a few years in Austria in the company of his sister, Mahboubeh Khanum and daughter, Guitty. He returned to Iran in 1966.
>
> Following his return to Iran, Eshghollah, having had training in Law while attending the Military Academy in Tehran and having served in the Iranian Army's equivalent of the Judge Advocate General's Office, turned to the legal profession, becoming an

---

129 Farshid Momen, in email from Guitty Bonner, 23 May 2018.

Advocate, as a means of supporting himself and his family. He went through a period of training in the legal office of Mehdi Amin-e-Amin, a close friend and one of the outstanding Bahá'í lawyers of his time before his martyrdom following the revolution. Eshghollah was a practising lawyer at the time of his death.[130]

In September 1970 (Shahrivar 1349), he married Nahid Ali-Akbari, who worked in his law office. She was not a Bahá'í. She was very kind to Eshghollah especially when he became ill.

Not long after this second marriage, Eshghollah was complaining of abdominal pain. Mahin remembers that he was getting frequent episodes of temperature. Mahin was worried about this and went to Zoghollah and talked about it with him. Zoghollah said that he knew about it. Mahin pressed him to do something about it. Then Zoghollah said that he has already seen a doctor who had said that it is cancer, but that this had been concealed from Eshghollah himself. The doctor had just said to him it was a disease of the bowels.

It was decided that Eshghollah go to Austria where Ida's husband was a doctor. Guitty joined him there. She writes:

> I have a love for sitting under the shade of trees in sunny warm weather (which sadly is infrequent in northern UK!). This I have adopted from my Dad from a precious period when we actually lived together for approximately 15 months with my Aunt Mahboubeh and her husband Mr Kouchekzadeh in Austria. I was about 11 years old. I recall a hot sunny day when my

---

130 Farshid Momen, in email from Guitty Bonner, 23 May 2018.

father decided to take his book and read it under the shade of a big tall tree in the expansive garden of the house we rented at the time, in a village near Vienna called Klosterneuburg. It simply struck me seeing him there in the beauty and tranquillity of the outdoors. It was a very peaceful scene. I believe my father loved nature and to sit by a stream or under a tree were probably a source of peace and joy to him.

Another time when I attended the English School of Vienna, again aged about 11 years old (and a very impressionable age), my father had bought himself a Volkswagen beetle to run around in. My school was full of diplomat's children who were driven to school in Mercedes limousines or similar, often by their chauffeurs. I was rather embarrassed by my father's old banger and asked him one day to park his car a little way down the road from the school so no one would see me getting into it. A day or so later he turned up in a red flashy sports car belonging to his friend, and parked it right outside of my classroom! I was so happy when I spotted him and waved from my desk. This was a more 'playful' side of him, a rare event through my eyes. I was really touched by his response.[131]

In Austria Eshghollah had an operation and returned to Iran. However, on his return, he complained that the wound from the operation kept discharging and he continued to have temperatures. Mahin tried to console him saying: "Well they say: *Dard kúh kúh míyád, mú mú mírih* (suffering comes in mountains and goes away by hairs)." When he saw that it was not improving, he went to England to see Guitty and Farshid (and receive further medical attention). Guitty writes:

---

131 Enclosed in email from Guitty Bonner, 12 May 2018

I do not recall him being sad, or downcast as he was always composed except for one occasion: Daddy had been in the UK to see if doctors could help in anyway with spread of the cancer. We had taken him to the Guardian's resting place at Arnos Grove shortly before his return to Tehran. On arrival, after difficulty walking, he mustered the strength to kneel at the threshold after which he immediately began to sob whilst offering his supplication. I was pleased he felt he could at last 'let go' where it mattered but it left another strong image I carry with me. Composure he regained again even when in the ambulance on the tarmac about to be taken to his plane to return to Tehran, and we both knew this was probably the last we would see each other. This is the saddest memory I have and as expected, he passed away shortly after his arrival. It was heart wrenching to wave him goodbye and to try and smile for both our sakes.[132]

On his return from England he had a nose bleed at the airport. Dr Forgani (Faramarz Farid's sister) said that this was now the end-stages and there was no hope. He was brought home and died a short time later on 27 December 1970.

---

132 Enclosed in email from Guitty Bonner, 12 May 2018

Zoghollah Momen

Zoghollah was born in Tehran on 17 February 1920 and went to the Tarbiyat School, where he was always top of his class. After this school was closed he went to the Military School (Madrasih-yi Nizámí). He then graduated to the Military Academy (Dánishkadih Afsarí). Because he had obtained very good marks, he was sent off to the Technical College (Dánishkadih Faní), where he trained as an air force mechanic, in the mechanical section of this College. He completed this college course which was two years and then began to work in the factory making military aircraft.

    Shortly after he joined the factory, Reza Shah made a tour of inspection. The previous year, when he had made this tour, Zoghollah and his friends had watched from the Dánishkadih which was just opposite and Reza Shah had got angry with the person showing him round the factory, a Bahá'í named Rawhaní, and had demoted him on the spot. This year everyone in the factory fled when they heard that Reza Shah was coming, leaving Zoghollah to show Reza Shah around. Reza Shah asked questions and Zoghollah answered them fully. He seemed satisfied and said to Zoghollah at the end of his visit: "Take care of these airplanes. Don't damage them. They are expensive."

    Zoghollah had only been in the college three months and reached the rank of Sitvan 3, when they said that it was necessary for everyone to fill in a form – and on the form was a place that asked for religion. In many of the sections of the military, the senior officer of the section did not care if the Bahá'ís left that section blank, but the head of the Air Force Mechanical section was a man called Khosravani, who was prejudiced against the Bahá'ís. He insisted that it be filled in. One day Khosravani called Zoghollah to his office to deliver an ultimatum and Khosravani's brother was there too. He said: "Aqa Jan! His Highness [i.e. the Shah] has said that in this place there should only be Muslims. If it were me and they said to me write 'Bahá'í', I would write 'Bahá'í'; if they said write 'Muslim', I would write 'Muslim'." Zoghollah said: "Well, each person is different." Many of the Bahá'í officers in the army were expelled in about 1940 (1319). On the official decree expelling him, it said that he was being expelled for lack of suitability – that he was not a sound person (*'adam-i saláhiyyat*).

The edict expelling Zoghollah was very strict saying for example that he should not be allowed to work in any government office and that all of his qualifications should be revoked. He was unable to get any work after this because the army had his school records and he could not get a copy. So one day, Sedratollah went with Zoghollah to the records section of the army. Sedratollah had his officer's uniform on. They went up to the clerk and Sedratollah asked for Zoghollah's file. The clerk found it for him. Then Sedratollah said: "Is his school diploma there?" The clerk looked and answered: "Yes." Then Sedratollah said: "Why is it still here?" And the clerk apologized and handed it over.[133]

A Bahá'í called Zabih (he later worked at the Bahá'í World Centre) who worked in the central office

---

133 Zoghollah Momen, interview, 21 April 2001

of the military, told Zoghollah that his file had come onto Zabih's desk and he had locked it away in a cupboard. Thus all of the strict decrees that had been made against Zoghollah were effectively negated.

After this Zoghollah worked for a time in the Bank Milli (National Bank) – because that was the only place where "religion" was not one of the questions on the form. He remained there for five years and saved money all this time. Then a friend of his suggested he work for a company that was building the Miyanih to Maraghih section of the national railway because the rates of pay were very high. He applied for the job and even though his potential employer was not there on the day he went for the interview, he got the job and went and worked for this company for some years as financial controller.

Zoghollah was able to save a lot of money doing this job and when it came to an end he began a company with Khamsi, Hushyar Ashraf, Nishati and a few others called Ahang Company and they sold refrigerators and other white goods. This was a very successful company and soon they had a number of shops open in the city. They were purchasing entire lots that Sabet was importing. Zoghollah ran a shop called Alborz at this time as a separate individual venture.

Zoghollah was the convenor of a 19-Day Feast in the south of Tehran. He was part of a group (*dastih*) of young Bahá'ís that included Ruhullah Samandari and his sisters, Iraj Ayman, Khamsi, Hushyar Ashraf and others. Bahiyyih Samimi and her sister Manijih occasionally joined in the activities of this group – she was a cousin of Ruhullah Samanadari. That is how Zoghollah and Bahiyyih met and they got married on 5 December

1953.[134] Bahiyyih's mother had been born in 'Ishqabad and had been expelled from there with her family to Iran. Bahiyyih's mother's father was Mírzá Mahdí Khan Askaroff Mutarjim as-Sultán, who had been a merchant in Ashkabad and had returned to Iran in 1913 and settled in the village of Mashhad Zulfábád, near Sultanabad (Arak). His wife, Bahiyyih's grandmother, was killed because of being a Bahá'í in that village in about 1917-18.[135] Bahiyyih was born in Zahedan, where her father who worked for the customs department was stationed. Zoghollah and Bahiyyih had two children, Dina in Tehran and Amin in Rimini.

Bahiyyih started with Mahboubeh and Gloria on the migration to England in 1955. She had only recently been married and was pregnant with Dina. She got very homesick shortly after they set off and when the party got to the border with Turkey, she remained behind there with a half-brother who was working there, then travelled back to Tehran.

A few years later, there was a general move towards pioneering and several of Zoghollah's partners wanted to pioneer. They had intended to all go to Brazil, but in the end Khamsi went to Switzerland where his wife's aunt was already. Hushyar Ashraf went to Rimini in Italy and when Zoghollah and Bahiyyih also decided to go, Hushyar Ashraf wrote to them saying: "Come to Rimini on your way to wherever you want to go. It is a nice place and you can stay with us." So Zoghollah and Bahiyyih went to Italy and liked Rimini a lot and decided to stay there. They rented a flat near the Ashrafs.

---

134 Zoghollah Momen, interview, 14 March 2004.
135 Avarih, Kavakib al-Durriyyih vol. 2, pp. 247-8.

He and Ashraf decided to open a shop selling Iranian handicrafts. Zoghollah went off to Iran to purchase the handicrafts and then to Germany where he had arranged to pick up a Volkswagen. He drove from there to England and took Kianoush, Shidan, Ida, Gloria, Moojan and Hooman on a trip to Edinburgh.[136]

In Rimini, Zoghollah opened the shop but it never made much of an income. So after a time he turned to constructing flats and selling them, which was more successful. Then one time at Kianoush's wedding, he met Kiani, who after talking to him there asked him to come to his office. There he made the proposal that he inject several million tumans into the company. So they went from making small apartment blocks of 4 or 6 units to large ones of 25 or more units. A short time later, Kiani had to flee Iran and came to Italy. Zoghollah felt that Kiani's intervention altered the balance in the company and there were problems with the scaling up involved. So after a time, he left the company and decided to return to Iran.[137]

When he went to Rimini, he had left Alborz in the control of two Bahá'ís and asked his sister Mahin to work there. Later he gave the company to the two Bahá'ís and after returning from Rimini, he started another trading company called Shirkat Farbáz.

A short time before he left Italy, he saw a plastic extruder machine and when he came to Iran he decided to set up a similar factory. He met two brothers, the Khosrowshahis, who had the same idea and had actually imported a machine for it. They agreed to form a

---

136 Zoghollah Momen, interview, 21 April 2001.
137 Zoghollah Momen, interview, 14 march 2004.

partnership and Zoghollah set up the machine they had. Soon they had to import many more machines and set up a factory in Karaj, because it was much in demand. The factory continued up to the time of the Revolution when it was seized. Even when the Revolution broke out, they had a contract with the Army to put up plastic wall coverings in a base in Chah Bahar in the far southeast of the country. His workers there phoned Zoghollah and said: everything is breaking down here – what shall we do? Zoghollah said: I have made a contract and I will fulfill it. So he got them to complete the contract and he submitted his notice of the completion to the government but of course his money was never paid.

In the early part of the Revolution, Zoghollah had responsibility for the Shirkat-i Nawnahalan for some two weeks. He had all of their books including the accounts of those who owed them money. The Revolutionary authorities were very keen to get hold of these books, but fortunately they never found out that Zoghollah had them and he had put them in the flat of someone who was abroad. So when his own things were confiscated, the books were not found. Years later, he handed the books over to Kianoush Kouchekzadeh to give to the National Spiritual Assembly of the Netherlands for safe-keeping.

One day, Zoghollah and Khamsi went to Tímsár[138] Rastigar who was in charge of procurement for the Army. They asked him whether he would accept a bid for a contract from them. He said: "Yes, I wish to God you would. The juniors in my department get bribes from the contractors, saying that they will share out the

---

138 Tímsár is a general title for high-ranking military officers.

money with the Tímsár."[139] From this time onwards, he and Khamsi were much involved in procurement for the Army. On one occasion he received an order for seven million pairs of socks. He had no idea how to fulfill this order, but he thought he might be able to do this in India. He flew there but he could find nowhere that could cope with such a quantity, so he had to pass on that contract.

In April 1979, Zoghollah made a trip to London from Iran at a time when it was becoming clear what a truly brutal and murderous regime it was that had come to power and how determined they were to eliminate the Bahá'ís. The whole family was gathered in Mahboubeh Khanum's flat near London, all of them urging and begging him not to return to Iran. "What is the point of going back only to be arrested and possibly executed?" they said. But he was adamant he was going back to face the darkness that was descending upon the land he loved and to help his friends. He went back and busied himself giving assistance and shelter to the Bahá'ís, many of whom had been dispossessed in their own towns and villages and had fled to Tehran penniless.

In December 1981, Zoghollah was asked if a meeting of the National Spiritual Assembly could be

---

[139] Years later, one day, when Zoghollah was in prison, Tímsár Rastigar was sitting in the window, reading a newspaper. On the radio the news came that a number of leading military men had been executed and it said among the names Rastigar's name. Rastigar was a distance from the radio and did not hear this. The others in the room who knew and much loved and respected Rastigar did not know what to do. The fact that the announcement had been made meant that they were probably going to come and execute him shortly. Anyway they were just discussing this when one of the guard came him and told him to go with him and he went. (Zoghollah Momen, interview, 21 April 2001).

held in his house. He agreed but as the Assembly were meeting, officials came and arrested the ten people present. Eight were members together with Farideh Rafat (who had come with her husband and was making tea for the Assembly members) and Zoghollah Momen.

They took them to prison. They were together for fifteen days. From the papers that were filled in, Zoghollah realised that he was being processed differently to the others. Anyway, a guard came in and blindfolded Zoghollah and said: "Come." They put him in a car and he did not know whether he was off to be executed or what was to happen. He reasoned to himself, however, that if it was a question of execution, then the others would probably have been executed before him. They took him to a building, took his blindfold off and pushed him into a room. There was no electricity in the room and it was lit with a *fanús* (oil lantern). There was no-one in the room from whom he could get information and the doors were of a heavy metal.

After a while he heard walking up and down the corridor outside and someone shouting at someone to keep silent. So Zoghollah banged on the door and when the guard answered, he said: "Do you have a newspaper I can read." The guard replied: "Do you think this is a resort? Keep quiet and don't bother me." So again he sat for a while. Then they said: "We are now going to lock the doors for the night. If anyone needs to use the toilets, do it now." At this point, Zoghullah heard the voice of Ginus Mahmudi, whom he knew asking for something and the guard (*qarávul*) saying: "It is not possible." From this he knew that he and Ginus were in this prison with other prisoners but he still did not know why he had been moved. They locked all the doors and went off. He knew that Ginus's cell was at the very end of the corridor on the same side as himself. He was trying to figure out a way of communicating with her. He got hold of the iron bars and pulled himself up and called out: "Brother, my name is Momen. I need to go out." But no sound came. So he called out again. Then Ginus called out saying: "Aqa-yi Momen: have they brought you here as well?" He replied: "Yes." She asked: "What news is there?" He said: "Nothing as yet. They are questioning me every day." She said: "Why did they bring you here." He said: "Because I was treated differently from the others and separated from them." She asked: "Is there anything you want that you do not have?" He replied: "I don't have anything." She said: "What about soap and towels, etc." He replied: "It is better if we do not establish contact." He asked her about herself and she replied that she was by herself there. So he would talk by grabbing the bars and pulling himself up and speaking and then lowering himself again. He also heard the voices of others. Someone was singing. These were holding cells not a prison as such.

    Zoghollah wrote the phone number of his office on the wall of the toilet with chalk. Ginus gave the guard a newspaper to give to him. The guard said: "Here the sister at the end has given you this. Is she your wife?" Zoghollah replied: "No. An acquaintance." Then the guard said: "She is offering you a towel and soap." She had obtained these things from home. But Zoghollah said that he did not need anything. It appears that since they did not have room in the other prison they had sent Farideh Rafat and Ginus here. They had then decided that Farideh was not of any importance and let her go. This was now about 15 days into the imprisonment.

Eventually Zoghollah was transferred to the notorious Evin prison where he was squeezed into a small cell with numerous other prisoners. They were so many that they had to take it in turns with one set sleeping and the other set standing and then the other way around. When eventually he was tried and sentenced, he was moved to the Qasr prison and then to Rajai Shahr and Qizil Hesar in Karaj. Here there were many other Bahá'í prisoners and they organized themselves to have educational activities. Zoghollah taught Italian and accounting. Other Bahá'ís taught English and French and other subjects. He was visited frequently by Majzoub.

When he was released from prison, he was still determined to remain in Iran and to do his best to help his fellow-Bahá'ís, even though his children were urging him to come to England and live with them. Eventually, however, his ill-health forced him to remain in England, when he was on a visit. He lived in a house by himself for a time but eventually had to live with Dina who took care of him during his last period of illness. He passed away in London on 4 December 2013.

Majzoubeh Behrouzmand

Majzoubeh was born 1924 in Burujird, where her father was working at this time. After her father's death, her mother took her to Tehran. She attended the Tarbiyat School for a short while before it was closed by the government. She then attended a school (*dabestán*) with Mahin which was very close to their house. After this, she attended Madrasih Shahdokht which was distant from their house and later Madrasih Navábagán, a private school, which was close by. Majzoub (as she was always known by the family rather than her given name of Majzoubeh) was married in July 1944, about three months before Mahin.

Mr Muhammad Behrouzmand was from Yazd and a businessman and merchant in the bazaar in Tehran. His original family name was 'Arab-Najafí, since one of his ancestors had come from Najaf to settle in Yazd. The family owned a business in Yazd weaving silk and other materials. They owned a large house which was both their home and also had rooms where the looms were set up for weaving. His family were all Muslims and his mother in particular was very pious. His father and sister died when he was still young and he had to help his mother run the business, becoming known to the employees as "Little Boss". He had been introduced to the Bahá'í Faith by a relative in Yazd, Mr Fání, and became a Bahá'í when he was 16 years old. As a result, his mother was angry with him and abusive and so he left Yazd for Tehran. There he was helped by Dr Jalal Rabbani to set up a business in the bazaar. When he told Dr Jalal Rabbani that he wanted to get married, the latter acted as an intermediary and introduced him to the family and to Majzoub. They married and lived at first in Aqa Muhammad Husayn Ulfat's house on Malek Road, where Nirvana and Sussan were born. About six months after Sussan was born, they moved to a house which Mr Behrouzmand purchased near the University, a good distance from the family home. When Mr Behrouzmand's mother heard that she had granddaughters, she established contact and came to Tehran, eventually moving in with the family. At first Mr Behrouzmand had a business in the bazaar but then he was introduced by Mr Kouchekzadeh to the publication department of the Iranian Parliament, where he worked until he retired. Nirvana Fleming writes of him:

> My dad was a wonderful devout Baha'i, he was kind, generous, he could be sweet, he worked hard to provide for us. He didn't like to drive, but he loved walking. The first time he got on a plane, to Germany, he fell ill and was hospitalized. He then came to the States and was with me for almost a year, but he did not want to stay, went back home and passed away couple of years later. My dad was very generous and he would help anyone, if he could. In 2007 when my Mom came to live with me, this gentleman would call Mom quite often from London. I found out that apparently my dad had helped him and his son sometime in the past; they never forgot about it. So the last time we were in London we met him at the Guardian's Grave where he volunteered in the gardens. He showed me a rose tree he had planted in my dad's name right in front of the

Guardian's Grave. I was touched and grateful for his kindness also.[140]

Majzoub was very good at making clothes. She made many of her own dresses and for her children and sometimes for her niece Nika. She also knitted clothes. She even made a coat up for herself once. She was a teacher of Bahá'í children's classes, which were held in her house. Nirvana Fleming writes of her:

> My Mother loved to sew and knit, she was very good at it. One year, I remember, that for Naw Ruz she made our dresses, coats, and matching handbags (I have a photo of it). This was one of the traditions of Naw Ruz, to have new clothes and new shoes, specially for the children.
> My mother was a very feisty go-getter. As little as they had at the beginning of their lives, she always got what she wanted. She was always busy, so my Dad bought her, her first Volkswagen. I was told, the first car she got, she had called a friend that day and told her, she would pick her up to go to their committee meeting. From then on there was no stopping her. She was a good driver, but [it was] terrifying to sit in the car with her.
> She was a great cook and loved to entertain. She had a heart of gold. She loved to help people in need, and during the bad times in Iran, she had at least three different people living at her home at various times. There was a Bahai lady of my age, who had an abusive husband, had no where to turn and her daughters and her immediate family would not talk to her or support

---

140 Account of Mr Behrouzmand by Nirvana Fleming in an email of 25 April 2018.

her. When my parents found out they welcomed her into their home, and she lived with them for several years. She was a nurse at a hospital, and eventually she got married again and moved into her own home. When I went to Iran in 2003, I met her, and saw the love between my mom and her.[141]

After the Islamic Revolution in 1979, life became very difficult. As well as the problems caused by the fact that Mr Behrouzmand's government pension was cut off, Majzoub had to cope with the fact that both her brother Zoghollah and her nephew Farid Vahdat were imprisoned and she would go and visit them regularly, taking clean clothes and other necessities. She was the only member of the family left in Tehran who was free and could do this. However, her activities helping Zoghollah, Farid and other Bahá'ís led to problems. Nirvana Fleming writes:

> Then two incidents took place. One time the police came to their home and took all their papers, books and some other items and locked these up in one of the bedrooms. Then they were warned that they would be arrested if they opened that door. Meantime during the revolution, I was able to talk to them on the telephone. Suddenly the Telephone lines to Iran were disconnected. We had no contact for about six months. During this time I moved to Amman, Jordan, and was working at the British Consulate. I met a gentleman who also worked at night at the telephone company. When he heard about my story, he helped me contact them. So after six months we were able to talk. My parents told me that when the the police came and locked all their books

---

141 Account by Nirvana Fleming in an email of 2 May 2018

and papers, they had also taken their small telephone book and they didn't have our telephone numbers.

The second incident happened one day when the police came to my parents' home. My dad was home and not feeling well. They took him down to the police station. They wouldn't tell him anything, or why they had brought him there. Then they asked my father, where his wife was. He would inform them that he didn't know. This went on all day, and at the end of a long day with nothing to eat or drink, they told him you can go home now, we are really looking for your wife, and we will come for her another time. This was their way to create anxiety and show their power of what they are capable of and more.[142]

Majzoub also assisted other Bahá'ís, giving refuge to some like Mr Vahdat who was being hunted by the authorites and other Bahá'ís who were trying to leave the country. Nirvana Fleming writes:

After my Dad passed, for over a six year period, two young Bahai girls stayed with my Mom at different times. She supported them while they were studying at the University of Tehran to continue with their education. Their parents lived in a distant part of Iran, and they needed a secure home and they didn't have a lot of income. Well they found a loving home with my Mother, who opened her heart and her home not only to them, but to their families. When one of these girls got married, at a later time, as a wedding gift, my Mother purchased a bedroom set and other household goods for them as her family could not afford a lot. At times their families would also come and stay with her for a

---

142 Account by Nirvana Fleming in an email of 2 May 2018.

month or so. When Mom came to live with me in New Mexico, she would receive many telephone calls from the girls, their family, and many other friends that she had left behind in Iran. They truly loved and respected her.[143]

Over the years however, Majzoub's health deteriorated and she needed to be with one of her daughters. So she left Iran in the summer of 2007. She travelled to Madrid, where there was a Momen family reunion to greet her, 29-30 June 2007. She then went on to the United States and lived with Nirvana in Albuquerque, New Mexico; she visited Sussan once for 2 months. She passed away on 12 August 2013.

---

143 Account by Nirvana Fleming in an email of 2 May 2018.

Mahin Vahdat [144]

Mahin was born 14 August 1927 (18 Mordad 1306) in Tehran after her father had died and so she never knew her father. Her mother was left with five children to look after and so she was helped a lot by her sister, Khalih Khanum (Khadíjih Ulfat), who had no small children of her own by this time. Khalih Khanum used to say to Mahin that she would take her to her mother's breasts to drink her milk but that she did everything else in looking after Mahin.

Mahin attended a school which was close to her home. When she first went to the school and she was asked her name, she did not know her surname so she made up the first name that came to her head – she said her name was Mahin Kumpani.

When Mahin was about nine, her aunt Khadijih Ulfat's son Jalal Ulfat, was transferred by his work (with the customs department) to Kerman and Khadijih Ulfat went to live with him there. Mahin had cried so much at this separation that eventually her mother had agreed that she could also go to Kerman. So she went to Kerman and lived there with Khadijih Ulfat, her husband Hájí Mírzá, Jalál Ulfat and her cousin Ruhi. Also in Kirman was her cousin Mihranguiz, daughter of 'Ali Ulfat. She was there until she completed her class 6 at the Zoroastrian School in Kerman.

---

144 All information from a min-disc recording made 24-25 January 2004 in Nika's flat in Madrid

She then returned to Tehran and started to attend the Madrasih Shahdokht with Majzoub but it was a long way from home and so they transferred to Navábagán School – a nearby private school, whose principal Mrs Badrol-Muluk Mawzun was a Bahá'í. She remained there until she had finished her class 10, when she got married. The school had up to class 11.

Mahin used to go to one 19-Day Feast with her mother and sisters and Sedratollah was the convenor (názim) for another 19-Day Feast (the Hasanabad area where Gloria Iman lived). Sometimes she and Majzoub would go to the 19-Day Feast that Sedratollah was the convenor of. Mr Husayn-Quli Vahdat was a member of this other 19-Day Feast. Mr Vahdat became acquainted with Mahin and he was a friend of Sedratollah because they had been to the Tarbiyat School together. Mr Vahdat made a proposal of marriage He sent Mr Ahmad Samimi and another time Ridvaniyyih Khanum, the sister of Dr 'Abbasian, who had taught Bahá'í children's classes at the Vahdat home, to Mahboubeh Khanum and other senior members of the family to make the proposal. At first Mahin refused saying that she was only sixteen and did not want to marry, but Mahbouibeh talked to her and said that this was a good man whom her brothers knew and vouched for the fact that he was a good person and a firm Bahá'í. So eventually she consented. The marriage occurred on 22 September 1944 (31 Shahrivar 1323).

At first they lived in Mr Vahdat's house in Khiyábán Estakhr in Tehran. After six months of marriage, Mr Vahdat, who was in the Accounts Department of the national railway company, was transferred to Sari in Mazandaran. There he was promoted, reaching eventually the position of head of the Accounts Department of the northern district of the railway company. Mahin returned to Tehran to have Nika delivered, and this was a good thing as she had a difficult delivery and her life was even under threat at one stage. Farid was born in Sari without any difficulty. Mahin's mother had gone to Tabriz to be with Gloria for the birth of Hooman and so Mr Vahdat's aunt came to Sari to be with Mahin.

Then in 1948 or 1949 (1327 or 1328), after the 45-month plan for pioneering was launched by the Iranian National Spiritual Assembly, Mr Vahdat wrote to the Assembly saying that they would like to go somewhere to assist with this plan. But they wrote back to say that they were needed where they were and should stay there. Mr Vahdat was on the Local Spiritual Assembly of Sari from the time they arrived there until they left after 12 years. When in 1333 (1954), women were permitted to be on the Assemblies, Mahin was elected the following year. She was also on the Youth Committee, the Committee for the Advancement of Women (which put on literacy classes and Bahá'í classes for the women), the Education Committee, and she was a teacher of the Bahá'í children's classes. Nika would be given an orange to eat and Mahin would get on with her work. Almost every day of the week, they were involved in some Bahá'í activity. There were about 70-80 Bahá'ís in Sari and many more in the surrounding villages. The village of Mahfuruzak was mostly Bahá'í and they had a Bahá'í centre there, which Mahin and Mr Vahdat visited. Mrs Qudsi Alaviyan used to teach classes in the village. One year, Mahin was elected by the youth of Sari as a delegate to the National Youth Convention. She and Mrs Tal'at Bassari were the only female delegates.

During the anti-Bahá'í campaign of Falsafi in 1955,

they were living in a house in the railway compund in Sari. Zoghollah, Bahiyyih and Mr Vassigh came to visit. The police advised the Bahá'ís to take great care and the Bahá'í Centre in Sari was closed after Falsafi's sermons on the radio. Bahá'í activities ceased for a time but they soon resumed once the excitement had died down. The Bahá'í Centre in Sari had been donated by Mr Hafizzadeh. It had a large hall on the ground floor and other rooms upstairs, where guests could be accommodated. Mahin and Mr Vahdat had stayed there for about 15-20 days when they first arrived in Sari, until they found somewhere to live.

Mr Vahdat had been having severe headaches for many years and the doctors were unable to help with them. Then in 1957 (1336), these became much worse and on one occasion he collapsed so they hurriedly returned to Tehran, leaving Nika (then aged 13) with someone in Sari so that she could attend school. Mr Vahdat was hospitalised immediately until his condition improved. His work transferred him to Tehran, where he was head of the accounts department for Tehran. He found the work stressful as he was very careful that no money should go astray and felt a great sense of responsibility towards his work. He retired from work in 1965 (1344) or 1966 (1345) and, at the suggestion of Zoghollah Momen, opened a shop at the beginning of Khiyábán Símetry near Khiyábán Sháh, selling refrigerators, televisions, sewing machines and other electrical goods. Although the owners of the neighbouring shop were prejudiced Muslims, they used to say "Mr Vahdat is a good and kind man. It is a pity he is a Bahá'í." To which Mahin would reply: "It is because he is a Bahá'í that he is a good and kind man."[145] He had one heart attack in 1962 and he passed away from another heart attack in 1970 (1349).

When back in Tehran, living in the house of Mr Kouchekzadeh on the upper floor, Mahin and Mr Vahdat were both on the Covenant Committee (*Lajnih-yi 'Ahd va Mítháq*), which was responsible for looking after the spiritual health of the Bahá'í community. For example, some of the Bahá'ís would have their shops open on holy days or do things that would bring the Faith into disrepute and they would try to persuade them not to do this. This committee consisted of about 8 or 9 people and included Mrs Malihih Bahar and Mr Durudkar. She was on the *Lajnih-yi Ma'árif Amrí* which would be for those youths who had finished the children's classes (*Dars-i Akhláq*). Mr Nasrollah Mavaddat, Mr Moghen, Mrs Mehri Afnan, and Mr Durudkar – about 8 or 9 in all – were also members of this committee. Mahin also taught Bahá'í children's classes. She taught the 5th class at the home of Dr Meshki and another class that was held in their home. The classes were of about 6-8 children. The districts for the children's classes would correspond to the districts for 19-Day Feast. A commission would pass on names for teachers to the Children's Education Committeee (*Lajnih-yi Tarbiyat Amrí*) for their approval. She was also on the Committee for the Progress of Women (*Lajnih-yi Taraqqí-yi Nisván*). Mr Vahdat was a supervisor (*názim-i sayyár*), who went around the children's classes checking on what was happening, and both he and Mahin were on the Bahá'í Education Committee (*Lajnih-yi Tarbiyat-i Amrí*). Altogether, they were busy with the affairs fof the Cause almost seven

---
145 Account by Nika Vahdat, in email 28 April 2018.

days a weeks. Later Mahboubeh Khanum came to Iran and sold their house, in which Mahin was living, and so Mahin bought the house of Gloria Momen across the road.

When Zoghollah was leaving to move to Rimini, he asked Mahin to go and work in his company Alborz and keep an eye on affairs there. Later when he returned to Iran, he gave that company to two of the Bahá'ís who worked in it. And Mahin then worked in the new company Zoghollah set up called Shirkat Farbaz. After the death of Mr Vahdat, Mahin looked after his shop for a time, but when it was sold, she returned to work at the Farbaz company.

Mahin made two trips to visit her daughter Nika in Spain. During the second visit in 1981 (1360), which had only been intended to be for a month, the situation in Iran worsened and she was one of the last Bahá'ís who managed to get out of the country by legal means (as far as she knows only one other person came out after her before the doors closed). She was thus forced to remain in Madrid.

After a few months Zoghollah was arrested in the month of Azar (November-December). Farid used to phone her every Thursday. Then one Thursday he did not phone. Majzoub phoned Mahboubeh and told her that Farid had been arrested and she did not have the courage to tell Mahin; she had said to Mahin that Farid had gone off on a trip to a small place near Isfahan and they did not have a phone there. So Mahboubeh phoned Mahin and asked how things were. Mahin said that everything was well but she was worried as it was now two or three days past the time that Farid usually called and she also mentioned what Majzoub had said. Mahboubeh said she would call Tehran and then she called back a few minutes later and told her that Farid had been taken for questioning and Majzoub had not wanted to worry you, because it was not of any importance – they were merely questioning him. With both her own son Farid and her brother Zoghollah in prison, Mahin wanted to return to help. Mahboubeh suggested asking Gloria to ask Mr FatheAzam about the wisdom of returning. He had said that returning would only lead to herself being embroiled in problems and causing problems for others. So she remained, living with Nika in Madrid.

Farid Vahdat's Imprisonment[146]

In 1362 (1982), Farid took it upon himself to visit some of the families of those who were under arrest. One day he went to the house of Mrs Farzaneh Mu'ayyad whose husband had been executed. The authorities had brought to her the blood-stained clothes of her husband. Mrs Mu'ayyad was very upset and weeping. She had a small daughter Roshanak 8 years old with her and her other children were in England and elsewhere outside the country. Farid offered to take the blood-stained clothes away so that she would not be so upset. So he wrapped them in a kerchief (dastmal) and took them home. As it happened he phoned Mahin shortly afterwards and told her about what had happened. Mahin said to him: "You must be very careful. If they raid your house now, they will say that you have killed someone." But Farid said that he could not take them back. So he hung on to them and even had to take them over to Majzoub's house, where she had a back-yard so that he could take them out and dry them because the blood was still damp.

Mrs Mu'ayyad wanted to flee the country clandestinely and Farid suggested that she take the blood-stained clothes with her since that was the best way to get them out of the country if she wanted to have them with her. She agreed and gave him the details of how to contact the people-smugglers who were getting

---

146 All information from recording of Farid made 25 January 2001 in Nika's flat in Madrid.

her out of the country. He contacted them and took the clothes over to a vanette that they were packing to go. He then returned to his office. They had his phone number. It happened that they were then stopped by the police and their car searched and the blood-stained clothes discovered. The police at first thought that they had killed someone as they were known criminals. So they had told the police that Farid had given these to them and they had Farid's telephone number.

The next day, early in the morning as soon as Farid got to work, he recieved a telephone from one of the people-smugglers saying: "Something has cropped up that I need to explain to you so please come over to our hotel so we can talk." Farid went over there and found himself surrounded by several people. They searched Farid and questioned him. Farid realised that things had gone badly wrong so he asked permission to pay off the taxi that had brought him. It was his usual taxi driver who took him to work every day, so while paying him, he told him to go to his office and inform them of his arrest. They took him to the police station (*kalantari*), which was being shared by the police and the *pásdárs* (revolutionary guards). He was put in a room. As it happened Houshang, the son of Mr Ishraq-Khavari, was also in the room, as well as a number of criminals.

The next day they began to interrogate Farid and it was the police who were doing the interrogating rather than the *pásdárs*. The policeman said: "As you are a Bahá'í, we will try not to create too much of a file for you, because if you have a big file and it goes to the *pásdárs*, then you will not escape their clutches. I have interrogated the others and so I know what went on. So I am going to write out your interrogation and your answers as well, if there is an error tell me." So he wrote the whole story out and Farid made a few small correction. He asked if he should write that Farid is a Bahá'í and Farid say yes. Then his file went over to the pásdárs. At this stage, Farid was still wearing his own suit although he had taken his tie off so as not to be too conspicuous. The pásdárs accused him of spying against the country, saying that he wanted to get the clothes out of the country so that it could be used in evidence against the government. They said that this a serious crime and he was to be held incommunicado (*mamnu' al-muláqát*).

So Farid was put into solitary confinement in a single cell. The door had an opening in it which they would occasionally open to check on him. The cell was about the size of a double bed. That night they brought in an Afghan as well. Farid asked him what his crime was and he said he had killed someone. The Afghan left after a few days and Farid was there for a week. Sometimes the hole in the door was left open and he saw that he was in a long corridor and through open hole in another door he could see a young man. They introduced themselves and realized that they were both Bahá'ís. His name was Fedros Shabrokh, a young Bahá'í who was later martyred. This was in the detention facilities (*bázdashtgáh*) of the Revolutionary Prosecutor (*Dádsitáni-yi Inqiláb*). Farid was interrogated every day and at the end of each interrogation he was left feeling weak and almost as though he was going to die. He would go cold all over. Serious accusations would be thrown at him and his explanations not accepted. The interrogator, who had obviously specialised in interrogating the Bahá'ís, would say that your case is closed and you are to be dealt with. Farid had resigned himself to a death sentence.

Then one night after a week of this, he prayed to the Báb and said a prayer which the Báb had said would lead to the meeting of one's immediate needs. He said this prayer 314 times and then asked the Báb to bring this interrogation to an end. Then he packed up his few things and waited to see what the morning would bring.

The next morning at 10.00 he was taken to the interrogator and told to get his things together as he was being moved. And he was moved to the Qasr Prison. Here there were some 20-30 Bahá'ís. One day he was looking out of his cell and he saw across the way in another cell Fedros Shabrokh. He later got better acquainted with him and the other Bahá'ís and they were all very firm and dedicated Bahá'ís. Apart from the worry of what would happen at his trial, he was fairly happy at this place. They held meetings in the evening when they would lay a table-cloth (*sufrih*) and some thirty or so Bahá'ís would sit around it. Prayers would be recited and some of the older Bahá'ís would tell stories. The other prisoners respected the Bahá'ís highly and if the evening meeting was late, they would call out saying: "It is time for your meeting." One of the Bahá'ís, Mr Varjavandi, fell ill and by the time the prison authorities got a doctor to see him, he had died.

The prison was one in which there were political prisoners and also the more dangerous criminals – those who had committed armed or violent offences. For some reason some of the dangerous criminals took it upon themselves to become the protectors of the Bahá'ís and, if anyone was disrespectful to the Bahá'ís, they would have to answer to these individuals. This was very useful as the prison population mixed freely and there were some very dangerous characters in the prison; knives would be drawn and fights would break out. The prison authorities learned of the fact that the Bahá'ís had acquired such great respect and they introduced a new regulation to say that no-one was allowed to communicate with the Bahá'í group as they were unclean (*najis*). They arranged separate washing and toilet facilities for the Bahá'ís. One of the prisoners was even punished for speaking with Houshang, the son of Mr Ishraq-Khavari. At the prison, Farid was allowed visitors and Majzoub became like a mother to him visiting weekly and and bringing clothes and other items for him and acting as an intermediary for messages to his mother and sister.

On one or two occasions, Farid was blindfolded, led off and made to believe he would be executed. They then said to him: "Tell us whatever you have to say or you will be shot." Then he was led back to his cell.

Also because of the coming and going of prisoners, they were able to find out about the prisoners in other prisons. So for example, Farid heard about Zoghollah's interrogation and warned Majzoub that they had asked questions about her and might be after her. During the six months that Farid was in this prison, he went to court twice. When he went to court, Mrs Mu'ayyad was there as well as the two people-smugglers and Houshang Ishraq-Khavari. They all went together before a judge (*qazi*), who gave an account of what had happened and gave his opinion on this. He was in effect prosecutor, defender, judge and jury. He then said that they had to return in a week when they would hear the judgement.

In between these two appearances at court, Farid was taken to the office of the prosecutor (*dád-sitáni*), where it was said to him that if he recanted his Faith, he could go free, otherwise his situation was serious. But

Farid replied that he was not able to recant the Bahá'í Faith as he saw nothing bad in it. A couple of days later he was taken again to the same place and again asked to recant and again refused. Then he was taken back to the court to hear the judgement. Mrs. Mu'ayyad, who had started the whole business, was told she was free to go. Farid was sentenced to one year imprisonment and one year suspended sentence. Houshang Ishraq-Khavari got ten years imprisonment. Farid was greatly relieved to finally know what his sentence was going to be after months of uncertainty.

Farid was put in a van and taken to the Qizil-Hisar Prison in Karaj where Zoghollah was also in prison. Farid said to him: "As you did not come out of the prison, I have come to join you here." He was in the same room with Zoghollah. The room had between 10 and 20 occupants and had two tiers of beds all the way around the edge. The doors were not locked during the day and so the prisoners could wander about the corridor and for a certain amount of time each day they were allowed out into the prison yard. Here as in the previous prison, the other prisoners were told not to associate with the Bahá'í prisoners. The block in which Farid was had just this one room of Bahá'í prisoners and the rest were all political prisoners. There were no other Bahá'í prisoners in Karaj. They would sit on the edge of their beds and eat their meals. Here the Bahá'ís had organised classes and Zoghollah was teaching Italian and book-keeping and others were teaching other classes. Mr Awrang, Farid's future father-in-law, was also among them and Dr Hakiman, Mr Sistani, who was almost ninety years old, who was on one occasion beaten very badly because he was the treasurer of some Bahá'í funds and they wanted to know where this money was.

One day they told everyone in their block to go into the prison yard. There was a great deal of commotion and much shouting. They were there from early morning until the afternoon. When they got back into their block, it transpired that there was a group of people who had been accused of being communists or Mujahidin-i Khalq and who had repented and converted to Islam. They had told these people to go into Farid's block and wreck it. They had pulled out everyone's clothes and all of the eating utensils and scattered everything everywhere. As a result of this, the prison authorities collected what they said was evidence against some of the Bahá'ís, including Zoghollah, that he was making alcoholic drinks (*sharáb*) in the prison. What had happened was that some people had put dried plums (*álú*) into water in order to eat these as a way of countering constipation. The prison authorities asserted that they had put these in water on the window-sill in the sun as a way of making alcohol. All of this material was sent off to the laboratory to be examined and everyone was questioned about it. After a time they dropped the charge.

A few days after this, they said that everyone in the block had to collect their belongings because they were being moved to another place. Farid had been in Karaj for about four months or four and a half months at this time. They were all put into a bus and driven to another block of the same prison. The prison was divided into sections and each section had about ten blocks and each block had some 200-300 prisoners. Here the more than 20 Bahá'ís were all put into a cell that had been designed for three persons. There had been three tiered beds along a wall, but the bottom bed had been removed so as to create more space and the room itself was about half a metre wider than the beds and half a metre longer. They spent the first day trying to work out how they could exist together in this space. They saw that some five of six could lie on a bed across the width of the bed with their feet up the wall. The first night they tried to sleep that way but they found that as they fell asleep, their legs would fall down and this would wake them. So from then on, two people slept on each bed – these would be the older people – and the rest would remain on the ground with about half sitting and half standing. Zoghollah was sometimes among those that was able to lie on the beds and sometimes sat on the ground. Those who were standing sometimes had to stand on one leg because there was no place for their other foot. Because the space was narrow, it was possible for those standing to put their head against the side of the middle bed and rest a little. They would then change over during the night.

This was a very difficult time. No sunlight came into this room and they did not allow them out of the room for the whole day. Their feet became swollen and inflamed and they all became very pale in appearance. Their meals were given to them in this room and only if they wanted to go to the toilet were they allowed out for a few minutes, after banging on the door and imploring the guards. People, some of whom were sentenced to many years in prison, also had some personal effect with them and there was nowhere to put these down so they were suspended with ropes.

They were all tired all of the time from lack of sleep. Even when Farid had a visitor, he was so giddy and tired that he would sit behind the window and fall asleep in the middle of talking to the visitor. Majzoub asked him why he looked so terrible.

For the first week or so it was like this but after a time they would leave the door open at night so that they could sleep in the corridor with the other prisoners. The other prisoners had been allowed to do this from the start, but not the Bahá'ís. Farid remembers his place was in front of the toilets and smelt. Even then there was not enough room for them to lie down flat. They had to sleep on their side like books. If Farid got up during the night to go to the toilet, he would have to push and pull to be able to get back into his sleeping place.

The prison governor and the guards were very annoyed if they saw anyone joking or laughing. The governor said that if saw anyone laughing, he would tear their mouth apart. They wanted the prison to be a miserable experience for the inmates and so the inmates were careful never to seem to happy near the guards. But despite this they were quite happy and laughing and joking about their predicament. After a little more time, they were allowed out into the prison yard for exercise for half an hour a day. With this, they began to feel a little better and the colour returned to their cheeks.

One day, one of the guards told Farid to gather up his things and he was being released. They gave him no time to say good-bye but as he was going Zoghollah said: "Give me your watch." So he took off his watch and gave it to him. Years later, the watch was posted back by Amin with a message that this is Farid's watch. He was taken to the prosecutor's prison and kept there for a night, where he was allowed to sleep outside in the open air. He was taken before the prosecutor and told that his year was complete and he would be released. He had been in prison exactly a year: six months in Qasr Prison, four and a half month in one block of Qizil-Hissar and one and a half months in the other block.

He went straight to Majzoub's house and she was amazed to see him there tapping on her kitchen window. She was overjoyed. After a day or so he was taken to his own house where the padlocks on his house were unlocked and he was taken into the house. There was a chest which had been locked and he was ordered to unlock it. But he did not have a key so they broke it open. Inside were some deeds to some lands that they owned but they left those alone. He was taken to the prosecutor's office a few more times and questioned. On one occasion, one of them said: "Now you have become an important person." Farid said: "What do you mean?" He said: "You have been in prison and have now come out again. You will be much respected." Farid replied: "Thank you very much for that."

Once he was out of prison, Farid used to drive some of the Bahá'í families to the prison to see their family who were imprisoned. He used to drive Mrs Awrang and her daughters to Karaj, where Mr Awrang was. So Farid came to know one of the daugters Haleh and eventually proposed marriage. Mr Awrang was still in prison at this time, but since he now knew Farid, he gave his consent. They got married and Farid's paternal uncle conducted the ceremony. They then managed to smuggle themselves out of Iran to Pakistan. After eleven months in Pakistan they came to Spain.

Family Genealogy: Descendants of Aqa Muhammad Husayn Ulfat ('Attar) and Fatimih-Sughra

This chart is laid out by successive generations. Each individual is numbered and their children are also numbered. If there is a plus sign before the number allocated to a child, this means that that child also has children and these can be followed up in the next generation – look for the number of that child in the next generation. Small superscripted numbers are generation numbers. These start with the parents of Aqa Muhammad Husayn 'Attár Yazdí (Ulfat).

Generation No. 1

1. **Áqá Muhammad Husayn^2 Ulfat** (Muhammad Mihdí1) was born 1853 in Yazd, and died 16 May 1936 in Tehran (26 Urdibihisht). He married **Fátimih-Sughra** abt. 1876 in Yazd. She was born abt. 1860 in Yazd, and died bet. 1936 - 1939 in Tehran.

Children of Áqá Ulfat and Fátimih-Sughra are:

+ 2 i. Khadíjih^3 Ulfat, born abt. 1877 in Yazd; died 23 Oct 1977 in Tehran (1 Aban 1356).

+ 3 ii. Sakínih Ulfat, born in Yazd; died abt. 1921 in Tehran.

+ 4 iii. 'Alí Muhammad Ulfat, born abt. 1882 in Yazd; died 16 May 1957 in Tehran

+ 5 iv. Vadi'ih Ulfat, born 1891 in Yazd; died Nov 1966 in Tehran.

+ 6 v. Muhammad (Mahdi) Labib, born 1894 in Yazd; died 14 Mar 1981 in Tehran.

Generation No. 2

2. Khadíjih³ Ulfat (Áqá Muhammad Husayn², Muhammad Mihdí¹) was born abt. 1877 in Yazd, and died 23 Oct 1977 in Tehran (1 Aban 1356). She married **(1) Áqá Mírzá Muhammad** in 1886 in Yazd. He was born in Yazd, and died aft. 1894 in Yazd. She married **(2) Haji Mirza 'Alí Ulfat** in abt. 1898 in Yazd. He died 1964 in Tehran.

Children of Khadíjih Ulfat and Áqá Muhammad are:

+ 7   i.   Jalál⁴ Ulfat, born abt. 1894 in Yazd; died 12 Jun 1965 in Tehran (21 Khordad 1344).
   8   ii.   Qamar Ulfat, died in aged 1 year old in Yazd.
   9   iii.   Diya Ulfat, died in as a child in Yazd.

Child of Khadíjih Ulfat and Haji Ulfat is:

   10   i.   Ahmad⁴ Ulfat, born abt. 1899. He married Rubábih (Mihrangiz) Dargáhí in Zanjan.

3. Sakínih³ Ulfat (Áqá Muhammad Husayn², Muhammad Mihdí¹) was born in Yazd, and died abt. 1921 in Tehran. She married **Hájí Mírzá Ibráhím Ulfat**. He died abt. 1938 in Tehran.

Child of Sakínih Ulfat and Hájí Ulfat is:

+ 11   i.   Dr Amínu'lláh⁴ Ulfat, born abt. 1899 in Yazd; died abt. 1996 in Brighton, England.

4. 'Alí Muhammad³ Ulfat (Áqá Muhammad Husayn², Muhammad Mihdí¹) was born abt. 1882 in Yazd, and died 16 May 1957 in Tehran (26 Urdibehest 1336). He married **Khánum Sultán Kirmání** in Kirman. She died 27 May 1958 in Tehran (6 Khordad 1337).

Child of 'Alí Ulfat and Khánum Kirmání is:

+ 12   i.   Mihranguiz (Mehri)⁴ Ulfat, born 1929 in Kirman.

FAMILY GENEALOGY 159

5. **Vadí'ih**[3] **Ulfat** (Áqá Muhammad Husayn[2], Muhammad Mihdí[1]) was born 1891 in Yazd, and died Nov 1966 in Tehran. She married **Muhammad Momen** 1913 in Tehran, son of Mírzá Mu'min and Shirin. He was born 1874 in Shiraz, and died bet. Jan - Mar 1927 in Burujird in late 1305.

Children of Vadí'ih Ulfat and Muhammad Momen are:

+ 13   i.   Mahboubeh[4] Momen, born 1914 in Tehran; died 15 Feb 1998 in Holland.
+ 14   ii.   Sedratollah Momen, born 1916 in Sabzivar; died 24 Aug 1952 in Tehran (2 Shahrivar).
+ 15   iii.   Eshghollah ('Ishqullah) Momen, born 1918 in Shahrud; died 27 Dec 1970 in Tehran (6 Day).
+ 16   iv.   Zoghollah Momen, born 17 Feb 1920 in Tehran (28 Bahman 1298); died 04 Dec 2013 in London.
+ 17   v.   Majzoubeh Momen, born 12 Oct 1924 in Burujird; died 12 Aug 2013 in Albuquerque, New Mexico, USA.
+ 18   vi.   Mahin Momen, born 14 Aug 1927 in Tehran (18 Mordad 1306).

6. **Muhammad (Mahdi)**[3] **Labib** (Áqá Muhammad Husayn[2] Ulfat, Muhammad Mihdí[1]) was born 1894 in Yazd, and died 14 Mar 1981 in Tehran. He married **Shawqiyyih** 1921 in Qazvin (1300 shamsi), daughter of Áqá Mi'márbáshí and Iran. She was born 1903 in Qazvin, and died 15 Mar 1993.

Children of Muhammad Labib and Shawqiyyih are:

+ 19   i.   Roshan[4] Labib, born 1921 in Qazvin.
+ 20   ii.   Parviz Labib, born 1922 in Qazvin.
+ 21   iii.   Sohrab Labib, born 1923 in Hamadan; died 1981 in Ahvaz.
+ 22   iv.   Freydoun Labib, born 1925 in Tehran; died 01 Apr 1996 in Colorado Springs, USA.
+ 23   v.   Irandukht Labib, born 1929 in Tehran.
+ 24   vi.   Mihri (Mehranguiz) Labib, born 01 Oct 1931 in Tehran.
+ 25   vii.   Firuzbakht Labib, born 1934 in Tehran.

160 MOMEN FAMILY HISTORY

    26   viii.   Jahangir Labib, born 1935 in Tehran; died 1964 in Tehran.
+   27   ix.   Munirih Labib, born 26 Dec 1938.
+   28   x.   Lily Labib, born 01 Jul 1944 in Abadan.
    29   xi.   Ihsan Labib, Adopted child.

Generation No. 3

7. Jalál[4] Ulfat (Khadíjih[3], Áqá Muhammad Husayn[2], Muhammad Mihdí[1]) was born abt. 1894 in Yazd, and died 12 Jun 1965 in Tehran (21 Khordad 1344). He married **Ruqiyyih** in Hamadan. She died abt. 1936.

Child of Jalál Ulfat and Ruqiyyih is:

+   30   i.   Rúhí Ulfat[5] (Ruhiyyih, Atá'iyyih), died 24 Aug 1979 in Tehran (2 Shahrivar).

11. Dr Amínu'lláh[4] Ulfat (Sakínih[3], Áqá Muhammad Husayn[2], Muhammad Mihdí[1]) was born abt. 1899 in Yazd, and died abt. 1996 in Brighton, England. He married **(1) Batúl Khánum**. He married **(2) Sakínih**. He married **(3) Irán Najmábádí**, daughter of Shaykh 'Abdu'l-Husayn Najmábádí.

Children of Amínu'lláh Ulfat and Batúl Khánum are:

+   31   i.   Viyúlit (Simin)[5] Ulfat.
    32   ii.   Iran Ulfat, died in in infancy.

12. Mihranguiz (Mehri)[4] Ulfat ('Alí Muhammad[3], Áqá Muhammad Husayn[2], Muhammad Mihdí[1]) was born 1929 in Kirman. She married **(1) Sohrab Labib** 1949, son of Muhammad Labib and Shawqiyyih. He was born 1923 in Hamadan, and died 1981 in Ahvaz. She married **(2) Mihdí Burhání** abt. 1970.

Children of Mihranguiz Ulfat and Sohrab Labib are:

+   33   i.   Sami'ih[5] Labíb, born bet. Feb - Mar 1950 in Kirman.
+   34   ii.   Mehrang Labíb, born bet. Aug - Sep 1954 in Kirman.

FAMILY GENEALOGY 161

    35   iii.   Farhang Labíb, born bet. Feb - Mar 1957 in Kirman. He married ? Johns.

+   36   iv.   Suhaylá Labíb, born in Kirman.

Children of Mihranguiz Ulfat and Mihdí Burhání are:

    37   i.   Bihzád^5 Burhání, born 1966 in Ahvaz.

    38   ii.   Mihrzád Burhání, born 1971 in Tehran. She married Mihrdád.

13. Mahboubeh4 Momen (Vadí'ih^3 Ulfat, Áqá Muhammad Husayn^2, Muhammad Mihdí^1) was born 1914 in Tehran, and died 15 Feb 1998 in Holland. She married **Jamshid Kouchekzadeh** 1933 in Tehran, son of Kay-Khuraw Kouchekzadeh and ? ?. He was born 21 Mar 1899 in Kirman, and died 31 Dec 1971 in Watford.

Children of Mahboubeh Momen and Jamshid Kouchekzadeh are:

+   39   i.   Kianoush^5 Kouchekzadeh, born 13 Apr 1934 in Tehran.

    40   ii.   Zhálih Kouchekzadeh, born abt. 1935 in Tehran; died abt. 1935.

+   41   iii.   Ida Kouchekzadeh, born 1937 in Tehran.

+   42   iv.   Shidan Kouchekzadeh, born 17 Jun 1940 in Tehran.

14. Sedratollah4 Momen (Vadí'ih^3 Ulfat, Áqá Muhammad Husayn^2, Muhammad Mihdí^1) was born 1916 in Sabzivar, and died 24 Aug 1952 in Tehran (2 Shahrivar). He married **Gloria Iman** 20 April 1949 in Tehran, daughter of 'Abbas Iman and Laqa'iyyih Hamidi. She was born 12 Dec 1932 in Tehran.

Children of Sedratollah Momen and Gloria Iman are:

+   43   i.   Moojan^5 Momen, born 25 Jan 1950 in Tabriz, Iran.

+   44   ii.   Hooman Momen, born 02 Apr 1952 in Tabriz, Iran.

15. **Eshghollah**[4] **Momen** (Vadí'ih[3] Ulfat, Áqá Muhammad Husayn[2], Muhammad Mihdí[1]) was born 1918 in Shahrud, and died 27 Dec 1970 in Tehran (6 Day). He married **(1) Jazbiyyeh Farzár** 1947, daughter of Enayatullah Farzar and Hoviyyih Asdaq. She was born 19 Nov 1919 in Tehran. He married **(2) Nahid Áqá-Akbarí** abt. Aug 1970 in Tehran.

Children of Eshghollah Momen and Jazbiyyeh Farzár are:

+   45   i.   Farshid[5] Momen, born 03 Oct 1948 in Rezaiyyeh (11 Mehr 1327).
+   46   ii.   Guitty Momen, born 22 Dec 1952 in Abadan, Iran.

16. **Zoghollah**[4] **Momen** (Vadí'ih[3] Ulfat, Áqá Muhammad Husayn[2], Muhammad Mihdí[1]) was born 17 Feb 1920 in Tehran (28 Bahman 1298), and died 04 Dec 2013 in London. He married **Bahiyyih Samimi** 05 Dec 1954 in Tehran, daughter of Gholamreza Samimi and Mithaqiyyih Mansourian. She was born 22 May 1933 in Zahedan, and died 07 Aug 1977 in Tehran.

Children of Zoghollah Momen and Bahiyyih Samimi are:

     47   i.   Dina[5] Momen, born 18 Jan 1956 in Tehran (28 Day 1334). She married Ennio Giordani 06 Jul 1990 in Rome.
+   48   ii.   Amin Momen, born 16 Dec 1962 in Rimini, Italy.

17. **Majzoubeh**[4] **Momen** (Vadí'ih[3] Ulfat, Áqá Muhammad Husayn[2], Muhammad Mihdí[1]) was born 12 Oct 1924 in Burujird, and died 12 Aug 2013 in Albuquerque, New Mexico, USA. She married **Muhammad Behrouzmand** Jul 1944 in Tehran. He was born in Yazd, and died 1997 in Tehran.

Children of Majzoubeh Momen and Muhammad Behrouzmand are:

+   49   i.   Nirvana[5] Behrouzmand, born 25 Apr 1945 in Tehran.
+   50   ii.   Sussan Behrouzmand, born 28 Nov 1949 in Tehran.
+   51   iii.   Ladan Behrouzmand, born 07 Apr 1954 in Tehran.

FAMILY GENEALOGY   163

18. **Mahin**[4] **Momen** (Vadí'ih[3] Ulfat, Áqá Muhammad Husayn[2], Muhammad Mihdí[1]) was born 14 Aug 1927 in Tehran (18 Mordad 1306). She married **Husayn-Quli Vahdat** 22 Sep 1944 in Tehran, son of Mukhtar Vahdat and Rubabih. He was born 1916 in Ishtihard, and died 23 Feb 1971 in Tehran (4 Isfand 1349).

Children of Mahin Momen and Husayn-Quli Vahdat are:

+   52   i.   Nika[5] Vahdat, born 08 Aug 1945 in Tehran.
+   53   ii.   Farid Vahdat, born 21 Mar 1952 in Sari (Farvardin 1331).

19. **Roshan**[4] **Labib** (Muhammad Labib[3], Áqá Muhammad Husayn[2] Ulfat, Muhammad Mihdí[1]) was born 1920 in Qazvin. She married **(1) Dr ? Mukhlis**. She married **(2) Dr Khalil Farhang Azad** in Abadan. He died Mar 1970.

Children of Roshan Labib and Khalil Azad are:

+   54   i.   Fariburz Farhang[5] Azad, born 04 Nov 1946 in Shiraz.
     55   ii.   Farideh Farhang Azad, born in Abadan.
+   56   iii.   Farhad Azad, born in Tehran.
     57   iv.   Fariba Azad, born 03 Oct 1962 in Tehran.

20. **Parviz**[4] **Labib** (Muhammad Labib[3], Áqá Muhammad Husayn[2] Ulfat, Muhammad Mihdí[1]) was born 1922 in Qazvin. He married **(1) Zhalih**. He married **(2) Gonda**.

Children of Parviz Labib and Zhalih are:

     58   i.   Gilda[5] Labib. She married Jerry.
     59   ii.   Peiro Labib. He married Sabina.

Child of Parviz Labib and Gonda is:

     60   i.   Paul[5] Labib.

21. Sohrab[4] Labib (Muhammad Labib[3], Áqá Muhammad Husayn[2] Ulfat, Muhammad Mihdí[1]) was born 1923 in Hamadan, and died 1981 in Ahvaz. He married **Mihranguiz (Mehri) Ulfat** 1949, daughter of 'Alí Ulfat and Khánum Kirmání. She was born 1929 in Kirman.

Children are listed above under (12) Mihranguiz (Mehri) Ulfat.

22. Freydoun[4] Labib (Muhammad Labib[3], Áqá Muhammad Husayn[2] Ulfat, Muhammad Mihdí[1]) was born 1925 in Tehran, and died 01 Apr 1996 in Colorado Springs, USA. He married **Frances**. She was born in Britian.

Children of Freydoun Labib and Frances are:

+   61 i. Farah Julie[5] Labib, born 07 Jan 1965 in Weehawken, New Jersey, USA.
    62 ii. Suzy Labib. She married Kent Norton.
    63 iii. Nini Labib. She married Bill Sigrist.

23. Irandukht[4] Labib (Muhammad Labib[3], Áqá Muhammad Husayn[2] Ulfat, Muhammad Mihdí[1]) was born 1929 in Tehran. She married **Parviz Anvar Na'inchi**.

Children of Irandukht Labib and Parviz Na'inchi are:

    64 i. Roya[5] Na'inchi. She married Del Kambel.
    65 ii. Kereshmeh Na'inchi. She married David Henderson.

24. Mihri (Mehranguiz)[4] Labib (Muhammad Labib[3], Áqá Muhammad Husayn[2] Ulfat, Muhammad Mihdí[1]) was born 01 Oct 1931 in Tehran. She married **Edward S. Molin** 06 Oct 1963 in Tehran.

Children of Mihri Labib and Edward Molin are:

 66 i. Lisa June[5] Molin, born 21 Jun 1965 in Taipei, Taiwan. She married Kent Yinger.

 67 ii. Eric Edward Molin, born 02 Nov 1970 in Taipei, Taiwan. He married Annette.

25. Firuzbakht[4] Labib (Muhammad Labib[3], Áqá Muhammad Husayn[2] Ulfat, Muhammad Mihdí[1]) was born 1934 in Tehran. He married **(1) Jan Whitney** 1960 in Portland, Oregon. He married **(2) Joan Kathleen Sheehan** Dec 1976 in Bergenfield, New Jersey.

Children of Firuzbakht Labib and Jan Whitney are:

 68 i. Jena (Gena)[5] Labib, born 1963 in Eugene.

 69 ii. John Labib, born 1966 in Hayward, California.

27. Munirih[4] Labib (Muhammad Labib[3], Áqá Muhammad Husayn[2] Ulfat, Muhammad Mihdí[1]) was born 26 Dec 1938. She married **(1) Stanley Hollenbeck**. She married **(2) Andre Lanzaro**.

Child of Munirih Labib and Stanley Hollenbeck is:

 70 i. Michael[5] Lanzaro, born 17 Nov 1961.

Children of Munirih Labib and Andre Lanzaro are:

 71 i. Joy[5] Lanzaro, born 17 Jun 1965.

 72 ii. Daniel Kashi, born 1961 in Ethiopia; Adopted child.

28. Lily[4] Labib (Muhammad Labib[3], Áqá Muhammad Husayn[2] Ulfat, Muhammad Mihdí[1]) was born 01 Jul 1944 in Abadan. She married **(1) Manouchehr Badii** 29 Aug 1966 in Tehran. She married **(2) Hassan Sobhani** 15 Oct 1993 in Houston, Texas.

Children of Lily Labib and Manouchehr Badii are:
- 73   i.   Chehreh[5] Badii, born 14 Jul 1967 in Masjid Soleiman, Iran. She married Payam Yazdanshenas 30 Mar 1991.
- 74   ii.   Chitra Badii, born 10 Jul 1968 in Tehran.

Generation No. 4

30. Rúhí Ulfat[5] (Ruhiyyih, Atá'iyyih) (Jalál[4] Ulfat, Khadíjih[3], Áqá Muhammad Husayn[2], Muhammad Mihdí[1]) died 24 Aug 1979 in Tehran (2 Shahrivar). She married **Sayyid Muhammad `Ali Ghiassi Razavi** 1949 in Tehran. He died 03 Jul 2007 in Namibia.

Children of Rúhí (Ruhiyyih and Sayyid Razavi are:
- +   75   i.   Riaz Ghiassi[6] Razavi, born 28 Jan 1950 in Tehran; died 13 Mar 1994 in Ciskei, South Africa.
- +   76   ii.   Razi Ghiassi Razavi, born 04 May 1952 in Tehran.
- +   77   iii.   Hami Ghiassi Razavi, born Oct 1955 in (Mehr 1340).
- +   78   iv.   Olia Ghiassi Razavi, born 12 Sep 1957 in Tehran.

31. Viyúlit (Simin)[5] **Ulfat** (Amínu'lláh[4], Sakínih[3], Áqá Muhammad Husayn[2], Muhammad Mihdí[1]) She married **(1) ? Firuzfar**. She married **(2) Amir-Firaydun Rasikh Qa'im-Maqami**.

Children of Viyúlit Ulfat and ? Firuzfar are:
- 79   i.   Firuzih[6] Firuzfar.
- 80   ii.   Farhad Firuzfar.

Children of Viyúlit Ulfat and Amir-Firaydun Qa'im-Maqami are:
- 81   i.   Farirokh[6] Qa'im-Maqami.
- 82   ii.   Fariba Qa'im-Maqami.
- 83   iii.   Amir Qa'im-Maqami.
- 84   iv.   Farinaz Qa'im-Maqami.

FAMILY GENEALOGY 167

33. **Sami'ih^5 Labíb** (Sohrab^4 Labib, Muhammad Labib^3, Áqá Muhammad Husayn^2 Ulfat, Muhammad Mihdí^1) was born 1946 in Kirman. She married **(1) Abbas Salahshur.** She married **(2) Booker Livingstone.** She married **(3) Frederick Labib Wood.**

Child of Sami'ih Labíb and Booker Livingstone is:
   85   i.   John^6 Booker.

Child of Sami'ih Labíb and Frederick Wood is:
   86   i.   Samira Labib^6 Wood.

34. **Mehrang^5 Labíb** (Sohrab^4 Labib, Muhammad Labib^3, Áqá Muhammad Husayn^2 Ulfat, Muhammad Mihdí^1) was born 1948 in Kirman. She married **(1) Imad Mustafawi.** She married **(2) Bo Day.**

Children of Mehrang Labíb and Bo Day are:
   87   i.   Francy^6 Donya.
   88   ii. Brenden.

36. **Suhaylá^5 Labíb** (Sohrab^4 Labib, Muhammad Labib^3, Áqá Muhammad Husayn^2 Ulfat, Muhammad Mihdí^1) was born 1953 in Kirman. She married **Bihbahani.**

Children of Suhaylá Labíb and Bihbahani are:
   89   i.   Gita^6 Bihbahani, born Nov 1971 in (Aban 1350).
   90   ii. Nima Bihbahani.

39. Kianoush⁵ Kouchekzadeh (Mahboubeh⁴ Momen, Vadí`ih³ Ulfat, Áqá Muhammad Husayn², Muhammad Mihdí¹) was born 13 Apr 1934 in Tehran. He married **(1) Parvindokht Quds-i-Jurabchi** 23 Feb 1961 in Tehran, daughter of `Azizullah Quds-i-Jurabchi. He married **(2) Jinus Azami** 17 Feb 1975 in Oegstgeest, Netherlands, daughter of Nosratullah Azami and Mahindokht ?. She was born 21 Mar 1951 in Khorramshahr, Iran.

Children of Kianoush Kouchekzadeh and Parvindokht Quds-i-Jurabchi are:

    91 i.   Ramin⁶ Kouchekzadeh, born 05 Jun 1965 in Cantebury, England; died 23 Apr 1976 in Iran.

    92 ii.   Mona Kouchekzadeh, born 19 Aug 1976 in Watford, England; died 23 Apr 1976 in Iran.

Children of Kianoush Kouchekzadeh and Jinus Azami are:

+   93 i.   Ramin⁶ Kouchekzadeh, born 02 Oct 1976 in Leiden, Netherlands.

+   94 ii.   Monib Kouchekzadeh, born 14 Feb 1979 in Leiden, Netherlands.

41. Ida⁵ Kouchekzadeh (Mahboubeh⁴ Momen, Vadí`ih³ Ulfat, Áqá Muhammad Husayn², Muhammad Mihdí¹) was born 1937 in Tehran. She married **Faramarz Farid**.

Children of Ida Kouchekzadeh and Faramarz Farid are:

+   95 i.   Gian⁶ Farid, born 17 Jun 1963 in Vienna.

    96 ii.   Ajang Farid. He married Parvaneh.

+   97 iii. Shamim Farid, born 21 Nov 1976 in Steyr, Austria.

42. Shidan⁵ Kouchekzadeh (Mahboubeh⁴ Momen, Vadí`ih³ Ulfat, Áqá Muhammad Husayn², Muhammad Mihdí¹) was born 17 Jun 1940 in Tehran. He married **Susan Jeffery** in Bournemouth. She was born in Bournemouth.

FAMILY GENEALOGY 169

Children of Shidan Kouchekzadeh and Susan Jeffery are:
  98 i. Vadiay^6 Kouchekzadeh, born 10 Nov 1975 in Bournemouth.
+ 99 ii. Vafa Kouchekzadeh, born 22 Feb 1979 in Bournemouth.

43. Moojan^5 Momen (Sedratollah^4, Vadi`ih^3 Ulfat, Áqá Muhammad Husayn^2, Muhammad Mihdí^1) was born 25 Jan 1950 in Tabriz, Iran. He married **Wendy Cunningham Wirtshafter** 12 Jun 1971 in Cambridge, England, daughter of Robert Wirtshafter and Carol Morris. She was born 21 Oct 1950 in Hollywood, California, USA.

Children of Moojan Momen and Wendy Wirtshafter are:
  100 i. Sedrhat Attar^6 Momen, born 14 Dec 1973 in London. He married **(1) Katie Maw** 1 Oct 2006 in Sheffield, England. He married **(2) Federica Ugliano** 31 May2014 in Torino, Itlay
+ 101 ii. Carmel Cunningham Momen, born 07 Feb 1976 in London.

44. Hooman^5 Momen (Sedratollah^4, Vadi`ih^3 Ulfat, Áqá Muhammad Husayn^2, Muhammad Mihdí^1) was born 02 Apr 1952 in Tabriz, Iran. He married **Monireh Obbadi** 20 Dec 1975 in Haifa, Israel. She was born 26 Mar 1950.

Children of Hooman Momen and Monireh Obbadi are:
  102 i. Saam^6 Momen, born 11 Jun 1979 in London.
+ 103 ii. Taam Momen, born 29 Dec 1982 in Rio de Janiero.

45. Farshid⁵ Momen (Eshghollah⁴, Vadí`ih³ Ulfat, Áqá Muhammad Husayn², Muhammad Mihdí¹) was born 03 Oct 1948 in Rezaiyyih (11 Mehr 1327). He married **(1) Louetita Josefina Ferrar** 23 Jan 1983 in Sydney, Australia. He married **(2) Goldokht Zayni** 27 Jul 1992 in Falls Church, Maryland.

Child of Farshid Momen and Goldokht Zayni is:
    104   i.   Neguine⁶ Momen, born 27 Nov 1993.

46. Guitty⁵ Momen (Eshghollah⁴, Vadí`ih³ Ulfat, Áqá Muhammad Husayn², Muhammad Mihdí1) was born 22 Dec 1952 in Abadan, Iran. She married **Frank Bonner** 07 Sep 1974 in Lincoln. He was born 21 Jul 1952 in Caistor, Lincolnshire.

Children of Guitty Momen and Frank Bonner are:
+   105   i.   Alexander⁶ Momen Bonner, born 13 May 1982 in Guildford, Surrey.
    106   ii.   Laurence Farshid Bonner, born 06 Jan 1986 in Ashington, Northumberland. He married Anya Charleson 12 Apr 2014 in Shetland, UK; born 11 Apr 1990.
    107   iii. Tali'eh Rosalind Bonner, born 08 Jun 1989 in Alnwick, Northumberland.

48. Amin⁵ Momen (Zoghollah⁴, Vadí`ih³ Ulfat, Áqá Muhammad Husayn², Muhammad Mihdí¹) was born 16 Dec 1962 in Rimini, Italy. He married **(1) Amanda Gordon-Harris** 09 Sep 2000 in Courmayeur, Italy. He married **(2) Gabriela Rosecka** 03 Apr 2010 in Adršpach, Czech Republic, daughter of Vaclav Rosecky and Marie Rosecka. She was born 19 Sep 1977 in Broumov, Czech Republic.

Child of Amin Momen and Amanda Gordon-Harris is:
    108   i.   Emilia⁶ Momen, born 30 Nov 2001 in London.

FAMILY GENEALOGY 171

Children of Amin Momen and Gabriela Rosecka are:
    109 i.   Emma^6 Momen, born 07 Sep 2010 in London.
    110 ii.   Max Momen, born 07 Nov 2012 in London.

49. Nirvana^5 Behrouzmand (Majzoobeh^4 Momen, Vadí`ih^3 Ulfat, Áqá Muhammad Husayn^2, Muhammad Mihdí^1) was born 25 Apr 1945 in Tehran. She married **(1) Farzad Ghaemi-Mahmoudzadeh**. She married **(2) Merton Rule Fleming**. She married **(3) Robert Allen Colby** 15 Jun 2001 in Albuquerque, New Mexico.

Child of Nirvana Behrouzmand and Farzad Ghaemi-Mahmoudzadeh is:
    111 i.   Dita^6 Ghaemi, born 28 May 1970 in Poole, Dorset, England.

50. Sussan^5 Behrouzmand (Majzoobeh^4 Momen, Vadí`ih3 Ulfat, Áqá Muhammad Husayn^2, Muhammad Mihdí^1) was born 28 Nov 1949 in Tehran. She married **(Robert) Kenneth Stratton** Aug 1977 in Memphis, Tennessee.

Children of Sussan Behrouzmand and (Robert) Stratton are:
    112 i.   Eric^6 Stratton, born 10 Mar 1980 in Tucson, Arizona.
+   113 ii.   Leila Marie Stratton, born 31 Oct 1983 in Tucson, Arizona.

51. Ladan^5 Behrouzmand (Majzoobeh^4 Momen, Vadí`ih^3 Ulfat, Áqá Muhammad Husayn^2, Muhammad Mihdí^1) was born 07 Apr 1954 in Tehran. She married **Volker Ebert** 05 Oct 1984. He was born 20 Oct 1948.

Child of Ladan Behrouzmand and Volker Ebert is:
    114 i.   Christian^6 Ebert, born 23 Apr 1986.

52. Nika⁵ Vahdat (Mahin⁴ Momen, Vadi`ih³ Ulfat, Áqá Muhammad Husayn², Muhammad Mihdí¹) was born 08 Aug 1945 in Tehran. She married **Juan Antonio Martin-Garcia**.

Children of Nika Vahdat and Juan Martin-Garcia are:

+   115   i.   Elena⁶ Martin-Vahdat, born 24 Jan 1967 in Liverpool, England.
+   116   ii.   David (Navid) Martin-Vahdat, born 01 Oct 1971 in Lorca (Murcia).

53. Farid⁵ Vahdat (Mahin⁴ Momen, Vadi`ih³ Ulfat, Áqá Muhammad Husayn², Muhammad Mihdí¹) was born 21 Mar 1952 in Sari (Farvardin 1331). He married **Haleh Owrang Hamidi** 18 Jan 1985 in Tehran. She was born 28 Mar 1964 in Isfahan.

Children of Farid Vahdat and Haleh Hamidi are:

+   117   i.   Nuria Nahal⁶ Vahdat, born 23 Jan 1987 in Madrid.
+   118   ii.   Lydia May Vahdat, born 28 Aug 1990 in Madrid.

54. Fariburz Farhang⁵ Azad (Roshan⁴ Labib, Muhammad Labib³, Áqá Muhammad Husayn² Ulfat, Muhammad Mihdí¹) was born 04 Nov 1946 in Shiraz. He married **Nahid Rabbani** 25 Mar 1972, daughter of Moosa Rabbani and Monireh. She was born 24 Jan 1946.

Children of Fariburz Azad and Nahid Rabbani are:

     119   i.   Shadi⁶ Azad, born 14 Jan 1975. She married Rolf Haag 19 Feb 2000.
     120   ii.   Shirin Azad, born 03 Dec 1978.

56. Farhad⁵ Azad (Roshan⁴ Labib, Muhammad Labib³, Áqá Muhammad Husayn² Ulfat, Muhammad Mihdí¹) was born in Tehran. He married **Shahla Parnia**.

FAMILY GENEALOGY 173

Child of Farhad Azad and Shahla Parnia is:
   121   i.   ?^{6} Azad.

61. Farah Julie^5 Labib (Freydoun^4, Muhammad Labib^3, Áqá Muhammad Husayn^2 Ulfat, Muhammad Mihdí^1) was born 07 Jan 1965 in Weehawken, New Jersey, USA. She married **Barry Hyde** 25 Oct 1997.

Child of Farah Labib and Barry Hyde is:
   122   i.   Zachary Frederick^6 Hyde, born 09 May 2000.

Generation No. 5

75. Riaz Ghiassi^6 Razavi (Rúhí Ulfat^5, Jalál^4 Ulfat, Khadíjih^3, Áqá Muhammad Husayn^2, Muhammad Mihdí^1) was born 28 Jan 1950 in Tehran, and died 13 Mar 1994 in Ciskei, South Africa. He married **Vera** 06 Feb 1978 in Maseru Baha'i Centre, Lesothio.

Children of Riaz Razavi and Vera are:
+   123 i.   Jalal^7 Ghiassi-Razavi, born 10 Feb 1979 in Roma, Lesotho.
    124 ii.   Ruhiyyih Ghiassi Razavi, born 08 May 1981 in Roma, Lesotho.

76. Razi Ghiassi^6 Razavi (Rúhí Ulfat^5, Jalál^4 Ulfat, Khadíjih^3, Áqá Muhammad Husayn^2, Muhammad Mihdí^1) was born 04 May 1952 in Tehran. He married **Sincere Vibangco** 18 Nov 1978 in Baguio City, Phillipines. She was born 07 Mar 1957 in Manilla Philippines.

174 MOMEN FAMILY HISTORY

Children of Razi Razavi and Sincere Vibangco are:
+ 125 i. Rezvan Ghiassi[7] Razavi, born 12 Sep 1980 in San Juan, Philippines.
+ 126 ii. Bahiyyih Ghiassi Razavi, born 30 May 1983 in Maseru, Lesotho.
    127 iii. Hediyih Ghiassi Razavi, born 19 Jun 1985 in Windhoek, Namibia. She married Nabil Wilf 07 Jun 2014 in Swakopmund, Namibia; born 11 Sep 1984 in Kuwait.

77. Hami Ghiassi[6] **Razavi** (Rúhí Ulfat[5], Jalál[4] Ulfat, Khadíjih[3], Áqá Muhammad Husayn[2], Muhammad Mihdí[1]) was born Oct 1955 in (Mehr 1340). He married **Qudsiyyih** 15 Dec 1988. She was born 23 Aug 1949.

Children of Hami Razavi and Qudsiyyih are:
    128 i. Vadia Ghiassi[7] Razavi, born 15 Nov 1989. She married Sipihr 24 Dec 2016.
    129 ii. Sana Ghiassi Razavi, born 13 Dec 1990.

78. Olia Ghiassi[6] **Razavi** (Rúhí Ulfat[5], Jalál[4] Ulfat, Khadíjih[3], Áqá Muhammad Husayn[2], Muhammad Mihdí[1]) was born 12 Sep 1957 in Tehran. She married **Eduardo Lopez** 09 Aug 1993 in Windhoek, Namibia. He was born 27 Mar 1951 in Cienfuegos, Cuba.

Child of Olia Razavi and Eduardo Lopez is:
    130 i. Jose[7] Navid, born 03 Dec 2000 (adopted son).

93. Ramin[6] **Kouchekzadeh** (Kianoush[5], Mahboubeh[4] Momen, Vadi`ih[3] Ulfat, Áqá Muhammad Husayn[2], Muhammad Mihdí[1]) was born 02 Oct 1976 in Leiden, Netherlands. He married **Nogol Rahbin** 17 Nov 2001 in The Hague, Netherlands. She was born 14 May 1980 in Uppsala, Sweden.

Children of Ramin Kouchekzadeh and Nogol Rahbin are:
131   i.   Kian Maxwell^7 Kouchekzadeh, born 12 Feb 2012 in Stockholm, Sweden.
132   ii.   Amin Colby Kouchekzadeh, born 05 Apr 2014 in Stockholm, Sweden.

94. Monib^6 Kouchekzadeh (Kianoush^5, Mahboubeh^4 Momen, Vadi`ih^3 Ulfat, Áqá Muhammad Husayn^2, Muhammad Mihdí^1) was born 14 Feb 1979 in Leiden, Netherlands. He married **Gabriela González Hernández** in Monterrey, Mexico, daughter of Francisco Martinez and Guadalupe Mendoza.

Children of Monib Kouchekzadeh and Gabriela Hernández are:
133   i.   Nina Shireen Kouchekzadeh^7 González, born 30 Nov 2010 in San Pedro Graza Garciá, Mexico.
134   ii.   Isabella Kouchekzadeh González, born 21 Mar 2016 in The Hague, Netherlands.

95. Gian^6 Farid (Ida^5 Kouchekzadeh, Mahboubeh^4 Momen, Vadi`ih^3 Ulfat, Áqá Muhammad Husayn^2, Muhammad Mihdí^1) was born 17 Jun 1963 in Vienna. He married **Corinne Schaubacher** 19 Aug 1988 in Berne, Switzerland. She was born 18 Jun 1966 in Berne, Switzerland.

Children of Gian Farid and Corinne Schaubacher are:
135   i.   Anissa^7 Farid, born 15 Jul 1992 in Pécs, Hungary. She married Arno Kersche 09 Oct 199 in Wesenufer, Austria; born 09 Oct 1990 in Klagenfurt, Austria.
136   ii.   Amelia Farid, born 03 Apr 1996 in Pécs, Hungary.
137   iii. Rene Farid, born 07 Jul 1998 in Steyr, Austria.

97. Shamim⁶ Farid (Ida⁵ Kouchekzadeh, Mahboubeh⁴ Momen, Vadi`ih³ Ulfat, Áqá Muhammad Husayn², Muhammad Mihdí¹) was born 21 Nov 1976 in Steyr, Austria. He married **Leily Saberin** 16 Aug 2002 in Bereldange, Luxembourg. She was born 11 Sep 1978 in Ettelbruck, Luxembourg.

Children of Shamim Farid and Leily Saberin are:
    138   i.   Shirin⁷ Farid, born 15 Jan 2009 in Luxembourg.
    139   ii.   May Farid, born 08 Jun 2011 in Luxembourg.

99. Vafa⁶ Kouchekzadeh (Shidan⁵, Mahboubeh⁴ Momen, Vadi`ih³ Ulfat, Áqá Muhammad Husayn², Muhammad Mihdí¹) was born 23 Feb 1979 in Bournemouth. She married **Azah Mentcheng Otia** in Northern Beaches (Sydney), New South Wales, Australia. He was born 11 Jan 1981 in Limbe Cameroon.

Children of Vafa Kouchekzadeh and Azah Otia are:
    140   i.   Abel Shidan⁷ Otia, born 30 May 2014 in Box Hill (Melbourne), Victoria.
    141   ii.   Mona Grace Skylar Otia, born 18 Nov 2016 in Upper Ferntree Gully (Melbourne), Victoria.

101. Carmel Cunningham⁶ Momen (Moojan⁵, Sedratollah⁴, Vadi`ih³ Ulfat, Áqá Muhammad Husayn², Muhammad Mihdí¹) was born 07 Feb 1976. She married **Ashley Southall** 28 Aug 2000 in Shuttleworth College, Old Warden, Bedfordshire, UK. He was born 23 May 1976 in England.

Children of Carmel Momen and Ashley Southall are:
    142   i.   Dreyfus Attar Darius⁷ Southall, born 12 Jan 2004.
    143   ii.   Aaliyeh Arora Fari Cunningham Southall, born 14 Dec 2006.

103. Taam[6] Momen (Hooman[5], Sedratollah[4], Vadi`ih[3] Ulfat, Áqá Muhammad Husayn[2], Muhammad Mihdí[1]) was born 29 Dec 1982 in Rio de Janiero. He married **Natalie Caroline Gibbons** 31 Mar 2007 in Ware, Herts., UK. She was born 07 Dec 1983 in England.

Children of Taam Momen and Natalie Gibbons are:
- 144 i. Anisa Obbadi[7] Momen, born 16 Dec 2014 in Kolding, Denmark.
- 145 ii. Ryan Obbadi Momen, born 29 Sep 2016 in Kolding, Denmark.

105. Alexander Momen[6] Bonner (Guitty[5] Momen, Eshghollah[4], Vadi`ih[3] Ulfat, Áqá Muhammad Husayn[2], Muhammad Mihdí[1]) was born 13 May 1982 in Guildford, Surrey. He married **Amy Athersmith** 10 Apr 2010 in Guyzance, Northumberland, UK. She was born 10 Oct 1981.

Children of Alexander Bonner and Amy Athersmith are:
- 146 i. Frederick Laurence[7] Bonner, born 17 Aug 2013 in Manchester, UK.
- 147 ii. Arthur William Bonner, born 13 Jan 2016 in Preston, Lancashire, UK.

113. Laila Marie[6] Stratton (Sussan[5] Behrouzmand, Majzoubeh[4] Momen, Vadi`ih[3] Ulfat, Áqá Muhammad Husayn[2], Muhammad Mihdí[1]) was born 31 Oct 1983 in Tucson, Arizona. She married Clinton Nathaniel Stibich 22 Jul 2016 in Rohnert Park, California. He was born 18 Oct 1981 in Vallejo, California.

Child of Laila Marie Stratton is:
- 148 i. Mackenzie Rianna[7] Stratton, born 10 Jan 2003 in Sacramento, California.

115. Elena[6] Martin-Vahdat (Nika[5] Vahdat, Mahin[4] Momen, Vadi`ih[3] Ulfat, Áqá Muhammad Husayn[2], Muhammad Mihdí[1]) was born 24 Jan 1967 in Liverpool, England. She married **Dariush Akhavan** 19 Jul 1990 in Madrid, son of Saeed Akhavan and Behrokh Boloori. He was born 11 May 1963 in Tehran.

Children of Elena Martin-Vahdat and Dariush Akhavan are:
    149 i.   Andre Amin Martin[7] Akhavan, born 03 Feb 1995 in Boston, Mass..
    150 ii.   Jasmin Martin Akhavan, born 02 Sep 1997 in Brasilia, DF, Brasil.

116. David (Navid)[6] Martin-Vahdat (Nika[5] Vahdat, Mahin[4] Momen, Vadi`ih[3] Ulfat, Áqá Muhammad Husayn[2], Muhammad Mihdí[1]) was born 01 Oct 1971 in Lorca (Murcia). He married **Judith Ann Korn** 21 Sep 1996 in Haifa, Israel. She was born 1975 in Alaska.

Children of David Martin-Vahdat and Judith Korn are:
    151 i.   Naim Alexander Martin[7] Korn, born 03 Nov 2004 in Madison, Wisconsin.
    152 ii.   Naomi, born 26 May 2001 in Madison, Wisconsin.

117. Nuria Nahal[6] Vahdat (Farid[5], Mahin[4] Momen, Vadi`ih[3] Ulfat, Áqá Muhammad Husayn[2], Muhammad Mihdí[1]) was born 23 Jan 1987 in Madrid. She married **Diego Gaspar Azparren** 25 Sep 2011 in Zaragoza, Spain. He was born 31 Oct 1985 in Zaragoza, Spain.

Child of Nuria Vahdat and Diego Azparren is:
    153 i.   Neizan[7], born 10 Oct 2016 in Ronda Malaga, Spain.

FAMILY GENEALOGY 179

118. **Lydia May**[6] **Vahdat** (Farid[5], Mahin[4] Momen, Vadi`ih[3] Ulfat, Áqá Muhammad Husayn[2], Muhammad Mihdí[1]) was born 28 Aug 1990 in Madrid. She married **Eloi Cirera Sant**. He was born 27 Aug 1991 in Sant Fruitos de Bages (Barcelona).

Child of Lydia Vahdat and Eloi Sant is:
    154 i.   Mey[7], born 26 Dec 2014 in El Vendrell (Tarragona), Spain.

Generation No. 6

123. **Jalal**[7] **Ghiassi-Razavi** (Riaz Ghiassi[6] Razavi, Rúhí Ulfat[5], Jalál[4] Ulfat, Khadíjih[3], Áqá Muhammad Husayn[2], Muhammad Mihdí[1]) was born 10 Feb 1979 in Roma, Lesotho. He married **Gholi Farahbakhsh** 27 Dec 2008 in South Africa, daughter of Manuchehr Farahbakhsh and Munirih Anvari.

Children of Jalal Ghiassi-Razavi and Gholi Farahbakhsh are:
    155 i.   Bahiyyih[8] Ghiassi-Razavi, born 23 May 2011 in Cape Town, South Africa.
    156 ii.   Bayan Ghiassi-Razavi, born 15 Dec 2015 in Cape Town, South Africa.

125. **Rezvan Ghiassi**[7] **Razavi** (Razi Ghiassi[6], Rúhí Ulfat[5], Jalál[4] Ulfat, Khadíjih[3], Áqá Muhammad Husayn[2], Muhammad Mihdí[1]) was born 12 Sep 1980 in San Juan, Philippines. He married **Vajdiyeh Shaker** 19 Dec 2004 in Cape Town, South Africa. She was born 21 Oct 1980 in Karachi, Pakistan.

Children of Rezvan Razavi and Vajdiyeh Shaker are:
    157 i.   Nazneen[8], born 21 Mar 2008 in Prince Albert, Canada.
    158 ii.   Aliyah, born 04 Nov 2012 in Prince Albert, Canada.

126. **Bahiyyih Ghiassi**[7] **Razavi** (Razi Ghiassi[6], Rúhí Ulfat[5], Jalál[4] Ulfat, Khadíjih[3], Áqá Muhammad Husayn[2], Muhammad Mihdí[1]) was born 30 May 1983 in Maseru, Lesotho. She married **Jean-Pierre Mongellaz** 01 May 2010 in Haifa, Israel. He was born 25 Oct 1980 in Chambery, France.

Children of Bahiyyih Razavi and Jean-Pierre Mongellaz are:
   159   i.   Maryam[8], born 15 Jul 2012 in Haifa, Israel.
   160 ii.   Chloe, born 17 Apr 2015 in London, United Kingdom.

Photographs

A. Tablets of 'Abdu'l-Bahá

هوالله

7138

ای ستمدیدگان محزون مباشید و مغموم مکردید و جگر خون مشوید دل و جان هر خردمند فهیما
و مسنان شد ولکن در ره جانانست و در سبیل دلبر مهربان گر در عطا بخشد یک مدقس دلها
در تیر بلا آید ایک هدفش جانها خانه و کاشانه هر چند ویران گشت ولی الحمد لله در حدائق الهیه
بر شجره طوبی لانه و آشیانه موجود و مهیا بنیان خاک عاقبت ویرانست و کامرانی این خاکدان
فانی نهایت حسرت و ناکامی پس چه بهتر از این که او مین بیوت در راه حی لایموت از نگاه
برافتد تا قعه شهید در ملکوت مجد مرتفع گردد پس هر لطمه در سبیل حق که بر وجود وارد شود
و سر مربتگی اعظم در ربه عفت و عصمت چه بهتر از این که در ره آن دلبر مهربان انسان نهایت
امانت بیند و رسوای عالم گردد نتیجه صون حمایتست و عزت ابدیه جهان رحمانیت
الحمد لله اسکوه نمودید مکه شکرانه فرمودید و علیکم التحیه و الثنا ع ع

طهران

الله الله فصیح ابن حسین عطار و سیل میرزا صالح محمد و میرزا محمد مهدی و صبایا الله فدیحه
علیها و غصن بهاء الله الابهی و الله رقیه و الله سکینه

Tablet of 'Abdu'l-Bahá addressed to Fátimih-Sughrá and her
children and comforting Fátimih-Sughrá for the humiliation she suffered in Yazd
in 1903 (translated on pp. 64-5)

Petition of Áqá Muhammad Husayn 'Attár Yazdí, addressed to 'Abdu'l-Bahá and naming his wife, all of his children, and grand-children.

Across the top of the page, 'Abdu'l-Baha has written with his own handwriting a prayer for the family (translated on pp. 70-71).

B. Historic Photographs

Áqá Muhammad Husayn 'Attár Yazdí (Ulfat)

Fátimih-Sughrá

With 'Abdu'l-Bahá in Haifa. Cropped from photograph on next page. Áqá Muhammad Husayn stands immediately behind 'Abdu'l-Bahá.
To the right of 'Abdu'l-Bahá in the photograph is Muhammad Labib and to the right of him is Dr John E. Esslemont who was visiting 'Abdu'l-Bahá at the same time.

Photograph taken near the shrine of the Báb on the occasion of a feast given by Husayn Ruhi, November-December 1918. Apart from those identified on the previous page, fourth to the right from 'Abdu'l-Bahá is Hand of the Cause Ibn-i Asdaq who travelled to Haifa with Áqá Muhammad Husayn Ulfát. Above Esslemont and slightly to the right is Lutfu'lláh Hakím; holding up the Greatest Name with both hands is Shaykh Faraju'lláh Zakí al-Kurdí.

Taken outside the house of ʿAbduʾl-Baha in Haifa, 24 October 1919. ʿAbduʾl-Baha is in the centre; Shoghi Effendi is at the far right of the front row. To the right of ʿAbduʾl-Baha is the Hand of the Cause Ibn-i Asdaq, between and behind them is Mirza Hadi Afnán (Shoghi Effendi's father); to the right of Ibn-i Asdaq is ʿAzizuʾlláh Varqá; between and behind them is Lutfuʾlláh Hakím. Áqá Muhammad Husayn Ulfat is in the middle row on the left of the picture, standing to the right of the man with the white turban wound around a fez; Muhammad Labib is the next person a short distance to the right in that row.

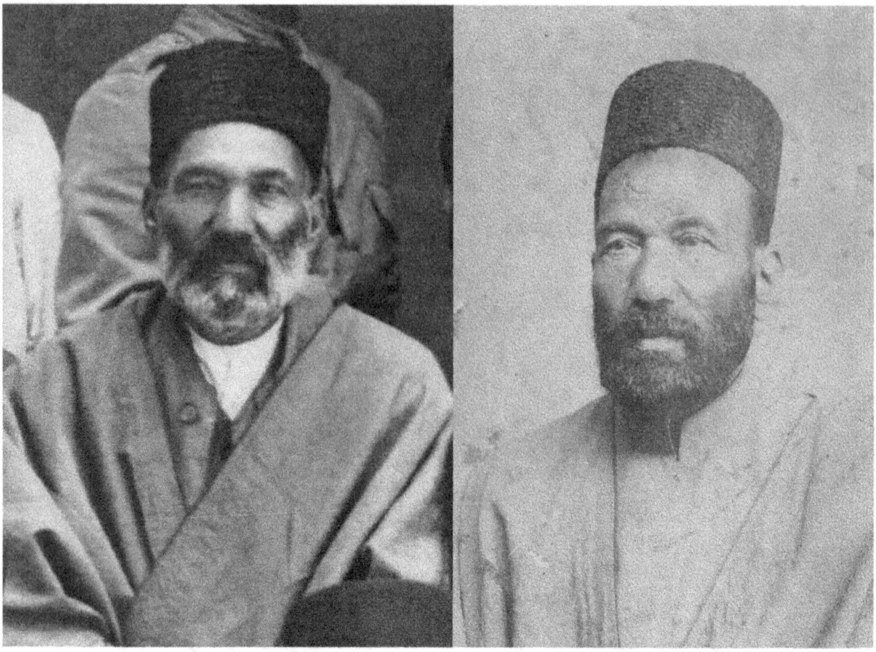

Áqá Muhammad Husayn Ulfat (picture on left was taken in Qazvin in 1917)

I. YUZD, FROM THE BAGH-Y-DOWLUT. [To face page 7].

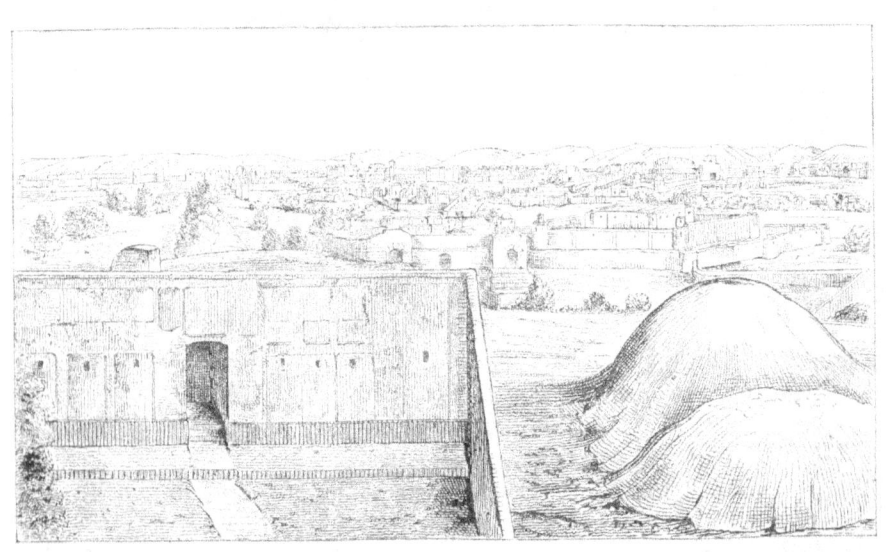

Yazd - View from Bagh-i Dawlat

Three of Áqá Muhammad Husayn Ulfat's children

Vadí'ih Momen	Muhammad	Khadíjih Ulfat
(Mámí)	Labib	(Khálih Khanum)
youngest daughter	younger son	oldest child

'Ali Ulfat,
Muhammad Husayn's older son

Photograph taken in about 1934. Top row, left to right: Eshghollah Momen holding Irandokht Labib, Sedratollah Momen with Fereidun Labib, Zoghollah Momen. Middle row: Ruhi Ulfat (Razavi) on left, Parviz Labib on right. Front row: Mahin Momen, Majzoub, Sohrab Labib, Roshan Labib holding either Firuzbakht or Jahangir Labib.

At the grave of Sedratollah Momen: Back row, left to right: Khanum Sultan (the mother of Mehranguiz, who was married to Ahmad Ulfat), Mehranguiz Ulfat (wife of Sohrab Labib), Mr Behroozmand, Mehrangiz (wife of Ahmad Ulfat), Mrs Habibi (friend of Mahin), Sohrab Labib, Vadi'ih Momen, Majzoubeh. Front row: Sussan (half face only), a niece of Mehranguiz (wife of Ahmad Ulfat), Mehrang (daughter of Sohrab and Mehranguiz Labib), Nika (in white dress), Mrs Habibi's daughter, Mahin, Nirvana, Ladan

Nirvana holding Hooman, Sussan, Moojan. In Áqá Muhammad Husayn's house on Malek Road

Family photograph on steps in house of Aqa Muhammad Husayn Ulfat From the top, right to left: Jalal Ulfat, Khadijih Ulfat, Mehrangiz (was married to Ahmad Ulfat), Mahboubeh Kouchekzadeh, Ruhi Razavi, Ida Kouchekzadeh, Muhammad 'Ali Razavi (holding Riaz) Shidan Kouchekzadeh

Vadi'ih Momen (Mámí) standing at front door of the old house of Aqa Muhammad Husayn Ulfat on Malek Road. In front of her is Nirvana. The other person in the photograph is possibly a street vendor.

Simin (Violette), Dr Amin Ulfat's daughter (Sakinih Ulfat's granddaughter)

Photograph taken in Davudiyyih 13 days after Naw-Ruz probably 1962 or 1963. Back row, left to right: Muhammad 'Ali Razavi, Mr Yadullah Navvabzadeh (Mr Razavi's cousin), Dr Aminullah Ulfat, Husayn-Quli Vahdat, Mahin Vahdat, Oranus Navabbzadeh, ?, Parvin Navvabzadeh, Pari Navvabzadeh (half face only showing). Middle row: Vadi'ih Momen, Olia Razavi, Sussan and Majzoub Behrouzmand, Farid Vahdat, Mehrangiz Ulfat (wife of Sohrab Labib), Khanum Modir Navvabzadeh, Ruhiyyih Razavi. Front row: Farhang Labib, Riza Razavi, Razi Razavi, Sohaila Labib, Ladan Behrouzmand, Jalal Ulfat. The Navvabzadehs were related to Mr Razavi.

Rezaiyyih, 17 May 1950, left to right: Eshghollah, Jazbi, Farshid, Vadi'ih, Gloria and Moojan. Sedratollah, holding the camera, had flown down with his family from Tabriz for a visit.

Family photograph, October 1951: Right to left seated: Vadi'ih Momen, Jamshid Kouchekzadeh, Khadijih Ulfat, Shidan Kouchekzadeh (kneeling), Sedratollah Momen (holding Moojan Momen), Jalal Ulfat (holding Riaz Razavi). Back row: Muhammad 'Ali Ghiassi Razavi, Mehrangiz Ulfat (Dargahi), Ahmad Ulfat, Ruhi Razavi, 'Ali Ulfat, Gloria Momen, Mahboubeh Kouchekzadeh, Mehrangiz Ulfat (married to Sohrab Labib).

Family photograph, about 1959, left to right at back: Ruhi Razavi, Husayn-Quli Vahdat, Mahin Vahdat, Majzoub Behrouzmand, Muhammad Behrouzmand. Seated on couch: Olia Razavi, Khadijih Ulfat, Dr Aminullah Ulfat, Vadi'ih Momen, Mahboubeh Kouchekzadeh. Seated on the ground: Sohaila Labib, Sussan Behrouzmand, Nika Vahdat with Farid in front of her, Ladan Behrouzmand.

C. Khadijih Ulfat's family

Left to right seated: Ruhi Razavi, Vadi'ih Momen, Khadijih Ulfat, Jalal Ulfat. Standing: Hami Razavi, Razi Razavi, Riaz Razavi, Muhammad 'Ali Razavi, Olia Razavi

Olia and Eduardo Lopez and between them, their adopted son, Jose Navid Lopez

Razi and Sincere Razavi

Bahiyyeh, Jean-Pierre, Chloe and Maryam Mongellaz

Hediyih and Nabil Wilf

Rezvan, Vajdiyeh, Nazneen, Aliyah Razavi

Family of Jalal Ghiassi-Razavi
Left to right: Jalal, Bayan, Bahiyyih, Gholi

Ahmad Ulfat and Mehranguiz (Dargáhí) Ulfat

D. Muhammad Labib's Family

Front row, Right to left: Roshan, Muhammad Labib, Shawqiyyih Labib, Fariba (daughter of Rowshan). Back row: Dokhi (Irandokht), and two daughters of Dokhi (Roya and Kereshmeh)

Back row, left to right: Parvis, Firuz, Jahangir, Sohrab,
Front row: Lili, Mehri, Roshan, Monireh

Front row, Muhammad Labib's daughters: Irandokht (Dokhi), Mehri, Monireh, Lili. Back row: Parviz Anvar (Dokhi's husband), their daughter Roya, their daughter Kereshmeh, Nirvana, Colby, Dell Campbell (Roya's husband).

Firuz (Firuzbakht) and Joan Kathleen Labib

Firuz (right) and his children: Jena (Gena) and John Nabil

E. Vadi'ih Momen's Family

Muhammad Momen's identity document

Vadi'ih with Dina 1956

Vadi'ih with Moojan September 1950

Vadi'ih's sons in back row: Eshghollah, Sedrhatollah and Zoghollah Momen. Seated: Ahmad Ulfat. In front: Kianoush Kouchekzadeh

Vadi'ih (seated centre) and her daughters, left to right: Mahin, Mahboubeh, Majzoub

Family reunion in Madrid, 29-30 June 2007:

Standing at back, left to right: Vafa, Susan, Shidan, Dina, Hooman, Guitty, Frank, Ladan, Nika, Farid, Haleh. Seated in middle: Carmel holding Aaliyeh (Lalli), Gloria, Majzoub, Zoghollah, Mahin, Nirvana. Seated at the front: Wendi, Moojan holding Dreyfus, Amin, Ida, Lydia

Madrid, 2007:
Left to right: Majzoub, Zoghollah, Mahin

Front, left to right: Shidan, Eshghollah, Ida. Back: Majzoub, Mahin

Family group in Tehran in 1949. Back row: Ruhi Razavi, Kianoush, Victoria Afshar, Mahboubeh, Gloria, Sedratollah, Mahin. Front row: Nirvana, Shidan, Ida, Tooraj Ayman, Nika

Front row: Ruhi Razavi, Shidan, Mahboubeh
Back row: Majzoub, Ida, Mahin

Photograph taken at Zoghollah and Bahiyyih's wedding, Tehran, 5 December 1954. At the back: Muhammad 'Ali Razavi. Next row forward, left to right: Ruhi Razavi, Mahboubeh Kouchekzadeh. Next row: Mehrangiz (was married to Ahmad Ulfat), Majzoub, Bahiyyih (the bride), Touba Samimi (Bahiyyih's cousin). Next row: Gloria Momen, Mahin Vahdat, Zoghollah Momen, possibly Jazbi Momen. Standing at the front: Moojan Momen, Hooman Momen

Family group in at Kianoush's house in Romford, April 1963 (at the time of the Bahá'í World Congress in London)

Left to right: Moojan, Gloria, Hooman, Mahboubeh, Vadi'ih (Mámí), Mahin, Farid, Majzoub

Same time and place as above. Left to right: Mahin, Gloria, Faribourz Azad, Muhammad Labib, Nika, ? (between Nika and Ruhi), Hooman, Ruhi Razavi, Moojan (crouching), Ida?, Mahboubeh, Husayn-Quli Vahdat, Faramarz Farid

At the wedding of Mojdeh Afshar and Shahram Mottahed, Royal Lancaster Hotel, London, 16 September 1972. Left to right: Kianoush, Parvin, Sussan, Gloria, Mahboubeh, Moojan, Bahiyyih, Hooman, Wendi

Family gathering when Zoghollah came to London in April 1979. Taken in Watford. Back row (left to right): Frank, Guitty, Moojan, Hooman, Amin, Farshid. Seated: Susan, Wendi holding Vadiay, Monireh holding Carmel, Mahboubeh, Zoghollah holding Sedrhat.

F. Mahboubeh Kouchekzadeh's Family

Wedding photograph: Mahboubeh and Jamshid Kouchekzadeh, Tehran, 1933

Back row, left to right: Mahboubeh, Kianoush, Jamshid. In front: Ida, Shidan

Kianoush and Jinous – wedding picture, 1975

Kianoush and Jinous, 12 May 2018

Left to right: Amin, Ramin, Kian, with Nogol at the back

Left to right: Gabriella, Nina, Monib, with Isabella at the front

Left to right: Ida, Leily, Shirin, Shamim, Faramarz, Ajang, May

Left to right: Anissa holding Shirin, her husband Arno, Rene, Ajang, Leyli, Shamim holding May, Corinne, Gian.
Seated: Ida and Faramarz

Susan and Shidan Kouchekzadeh, March 2011

Vadiay Kouchekzadeh

Left to right: Azah, Abel, Vafa, and Mona Otia

G. Sedratollah Momen's Family

Wedding photograph: Sedratollah and Gloria

Sedratollah, Moojan, Vadi'ih in Tabriz 1952

Photograph taken at Shah-Quli, Tabriz, May 1952 Left to right: Ruha (holding Hooman), Vadi'ih, Moojan, Gloria.

Moojan, Gloria, Hooman

Hooman and Moojan on first day at school in Bournemouth, England, 21 September 1955

Taam and Saam in about 1980

Moojan and Wendi's wedding photograph 12 June 1971

Photograph taken at Acuto, Italy, 2016. Back: left to right: Federica, Sedrhat, Carmel, Ashley, Saam, Natalie, Taam. Front: Wendi, Moojan, Aaliyeh (Lalli), Gloria, Dreyfus, Hooman, Monireh with Anisa

Back: Dreyfus, Carmel, Ashley, Wendi, Sedrhat. Front: Aaliyeh (Lalli), Moojan

Wedding photograph: Sedrhat and Federica Momen, 31 May 2014

Carmel, Aaliyeh (Lalli), Ashley, Dreyfus, taken in Manchester, 31 July 2017

Hooman and Monireh

Taam, Natalie, Anisa and Ryan Momen

Saam Momen

H. Eshghollah Momen's Family

Left to right: Guitty, Eshghollah, Farshid with Jazbi'eh at back

Photograph taken when members of the Iran National Spiritual Assembly visited Reza'iyyih (Urumiyyih), on the occasion of the centenary of the Martyrdom of the Bab, 1950. Back row: left to right: Mr Afsahi, ?, Nurud-Din FatheAzam, Yadullah Zabih. Middle Row: Mr Niknam, Valiyullah Varqa, Col. 'Ala'i, Eshghollah Momen (chairman of Reza'iyyih Local Spritual Assembly, holding the Greatest Name), 'Ali Akbar Furutan, Nurullah Jasbi, Mr Husaynzadih. Front row: Zikrullah Khadem, Ali Nakhjavani, Dr Masih Farhangi, Dr Ishraqi.

Farshid, Neguine, Goli in 2017

Guitty and Frank Bonner – wedding photo, Lincoln, 7 September 1974

Bonner family, left to right, back row: Alexander, Amy, Guitty, Frank.
Front row: Tali'eh, Anya, Laurence

Laurence and Anya Bonner

Guitty and Frank,
Great Whittington,
Northumberland,
July 2012

Freddie (Frederick) and Arthur Bonner

I. Zoghollah Momen's Family

Bahiyyih and Zoghollah – wedding photograph, Tehran,
5 December 1954

Left to right: Zoghollah, Amin, Bahiyyih, Dina, Mithaqiyyih
Samini (Bahiyyih's mother)

Zoghollah, Spring 1993, Tehran

Left to right: Max, Emma and Dina

Dina, Amin, Emilia, 2010

Gabriella, Amin, Emilia, with Max and Emma in front, Rhodes, August 2017

J. Majzoubeh Behrouzmand's Family

Majzoubeh and Muhammad Behrouzmand

First there was Nirvana . . .

then there was Nirvana and Sussan

. . . then there was Nirvana, Sussan and Ladan

Seated outside the Kouchekzadeh house, left to right: Sussan, Nirvana, Majzoub (pregnant with Ladan)

Ladan, Christian and Volker Ebert

Left to right: Majzoub, Christian, Ladan and Nirvana in Tehran

Majzoub with her daughters.
Left to right: Sussan, Majzoub, Nirvana, Ladan

Majzoub with her grandchildren.
Left to right: Dita, Christian, Mazoub, Eric, Leila

Nirvana and Dita

Mackenzie and Leila

K. Mahin Vahdat's Family

Mahin and Husayn-Qoli Vahdat
Wedding photograph,
22 September 1944

Mahin, Husayn-Qoli, Nika and Farid

Mahin (behind) looked after both Vadi'ih (left) and Khadijih (right) when they grew old

Nika, Mahin, and Farid Vahdat

Left to right: Andre, Dariush, Elena, Nika, David (Navid) holding Naim, Jasmin, Judith holding Naomi

Photograph taken May 2018. Left to right: Eloi holding Mey, Lydia, Farid, Nuria, Diego holding Neizan.
Both Nuria and Lydia are expecting their second child in this photograph.

Dariush, Jasmin, Elena, Andre

Photograph taken 2017. Left to right: Naim, David (Navid), Judith, Naomi

L. Miscellaneous photographs

August 1955: Arrival of Mahboubeh, Gloria, Moojan and Hooman in London (from Iran). Shidan who is probably taking the photograph came with them. Ida (at left) and Kianoush (at right) were already in England

In the roof-garden at Derry and Toms, London – September 1955
Gloria, Hooman, Mahboubeh, Ida, Kianoush, Moojan

Mahboubeh and Jamshid Kouchekzadeh, standing outside their residence in Ranelagh, Dublin, with Moojan and Hooman, 15 August 1959

On the road to Edinburgh, about 1957. All those in this picture, together with Shidan who is taking the picture were squeezed into Zoghollah's Volkswagen Beetle with Hooman and Moojan in the luggage compartment behind the back seat and the luggage in the bonnet and on the roof. Left to right: Gloria, Moojan, Kianoush, Ida, Hooman, Zoghollah

Tehran, Summer 1970, at the Behrouzmand home, left to right: Sussan, Farid, Ladan, Majzoub, Nirvana, Peter Smith, Moojan holding Dita

Taken in London in January 2010 at Moojan's 60th birthday party. These were all the males with the surname of Momen in the family at this time (except Farshid). Front, left to right: Hooman, Zoghollah, Moojan, Sedrhat. Back: Amin, Saam, Taam

Nika, Gloria, and Moojan outside 10a Glen Road, Bournemouth. Gloria and family lived in upper floor flat. This is where Shidan and Susan were married.

Taken at Amin's house in London, 1994. Shortly after Zoghollah was released from prison, there was a family get-together to greet him. Back row, left to right: Sedrhat, Gloria, Susan, Moojan, Carmel, Vadiay, Vafa, Shidan, Farid. Front row: Zoghollah, Mahboubeh, Mahin

Family gathering at the home of Moojan and Wendi Momen, 29 August 2004, left to right at back: Wendi, Ashley, Kate, Sedrhat, Frank, Tali'eh, Zoghollah, Guitty, Carmel holding Dreyfus, Gloria. At front: Moojan, Amin, Taam

The Cousins gathered at Madrid in June 2007. Back row, left to right: Guitty, Shidan, Farid, Dina, Hooman, Moojan. Front Row: Amin, Nika, Nirvana, Ida, Ladan. Only three of the cousins are missing: Kianoush, Farshid and Sussan

Family gathering in Munich, 28 August 2005. Left to right: Monireh, Shidan, Ladan, Christian, Sussan, Ida, Majzoub, Maria Cecilia Gomes Barreira (Monireh's friend from Brazil), Susan, Colby, Nirvana, Faramarz, Hooman. Photograph taken by Moojan.

Family gathering at Dina's house for Zoghollah's 90th birthday, February 2012. Back row, left to right: Dina, Moojan, Christian, Taam, Gabriela, Laurence, Alexander, Susan, Shidan. Middle row, seated on couch: Zoghollah, Mahin, Guitty, Nika, Ladan, Hooman. Front row: Wendi, Amin, Emilia, Carmel holding Aaliyeh (Lalli), Sedrhat holding Dreyfus, Natalie, Ashley.

www.ingramcontent.com/pod-product-compliance
Lightning Source LLC
Chambersburg PA
CBHW050630300426
44112CB00012B/1743